Illustrator 8.0

FOR MACINTOSH AND WINDOWS

Christopher Lumgair

TEACH YOURSELF BOOKS

For UK orders: please contact Bookpoint Ltd, 39 Milton Park, Abingdon, Oxon OX14 4TD. Telephone: (44) (0)1235 400414, Fax: (44) (0)1235 400454. Lines are open 9.00–6.00, Monday to Saturday, with a 24-hour message answering service. Email address: orders@bookpoint.co.uk.

For USA & Canada orders: please contact NTC/Contemporary Publishing, 4255 West Touhy Avenue, Lincolnwood, Illinois 60646 –1975, USA Telephone: (847) 679 5500, Fax: (847) 679 2494.

Long renowned as the authoritative source of self-guided learning – with more than 40 million copies sold worldwide – the *Teach Yourself* series includes over 200 titles in the fields of languages, crafts, hobbies, business and education.

A catalogue record for this title is available from The British Library.

Library of Congress Catalog Card Number: On file

First published in UK 1999 by Hodder Headline Plc, 338 Euston Road, London NW1 3BH.

First published in US 1999 by NTC/Contemporary Publishing Company, 4255 West Touhy Avenue, Lincolnwood (Chicago), Illinois 60646 –1975, USA.

The 'Teach Yourself' name and logo are registered trade marks of Hodder & Stoughton Ltd.

Printed in Great Britain for Hodder & Stoughton Educational, a division of Hodder Headline Plc, 338 Euston Road, London NW1 3BH, by Cox & Wyman Ltd, Reading, Berkshire.

Impression number	12	11	10	9	8	7	6	5	4	3	2	1
Year		2004	2003		2002	2001	2000	1999				

CONTENTS

1 | INTRODUCTION

This book has a simple purpose: to introduce complete beginners to vector drawing using Adobe Illustrator 8.0 for Macintosh and Windows and to teach the necessary skills to create, edit and compose artworks with a degree of confidence.

In aiming to give readers a good grounding in the use of the program, I have concentrated on those essential controls, techniques and processes required in artwork production.

Whilst many of the chapters are devoted to specific tasks, such as painting in colour and transforming objects, in one chapter I cover a mix of techniques, each addressing a particular artwork effect. Key properties such as transparency, patterns and colour blending are covered in detail in the context of real-life examples.

Illustrator is often used solely for its graph creation facility. Though space precludes me from devoting more than a chapter to the subject, I trust that the coverage I give inspires you to further explore the program's graphing potential.

Multimedia in all its manifestations has meant that the computer has become a medium in its own right rather than just a tool. Digital artworks are now as likely to be integrated into web pages and multimedia projects as into DTP documents and I have kept this in mind whilst writing this book.

Whether you are new to visual communications or already work in the graphic arts field, I hope you will find this a useful guide to a remarkable drawing and layout tool.

Please e-mail me at studio@clara.net if you have any comments.

Overview of Illustrator

What is Illustrator?

Illustrator is a drawing and layout program, providing the user with a single environment in which illustrations, graphics, graphs and artwork can be accomplished.

It includes:
    artboard controls and guides
    drawing and editing tools
    colour controls
    editing operations
    layer and transformation controls
    compounding, blending, pattern and mask controls
    graph and type controls
    bitmapping and effect filters
    outputting and exporting capabilities.

Draw images

Draw, vector or object-oriented images as they are variously called comprise mathematically defined PostScript objects, each object representing a single entity within an artwork, whether it's an illustration or a layout. Objects have a dimension and direction associated with them, as well as line widths (called strokes) and fill colours and/or patterns.

The artboard

Artworks are created within a resizeable area representing a traditional artboard. You can add guides of various sorts to the artboard for accurate object positioning. Printing areas can also be delineated as page tiling.

Drawing and editing

You can create objects as simple shapes or hand plot them. Either way object paths can be edited at will until the desired forms are achieved. Objects can also be automatically created from placed images.

Colour

Objects can be coloured in several ways. They can be chosen from colour libraries or mixed from a number of spaces/palettes to suit different media. They can also be specified as process or spot and trapped to allow for print misregistration. Accurate on-screen colour is taken care of by a colour management system and a monitor calibration regime.

Editing operations

Heavy duty editing involving the combining, dividing, merging and cropping of objects is facilitated by special Pathfinder filters; stylistic modifications to paths can also be made using special effect filters.

Layers and transformations

Artwork can be separated into layers for ease of object selection and to aid visualization. Objects can be transformed in a number of ways including rotating, flipping, scaling and shearing.

Compounding, blending, patterns and masks

You can compound objects to create transparency and blend them to create object-based gradients and intermediary objects. You can also create repeat patterns based on your designs and hide objects using masks.

Graphs and type

Graphs can be automatically generated from data in one of eight graph types, with columns and markers of your own design incorporated as required. You can enter and format type in documents in a number of ways. Type can be made to follow a path or fill a shape. It can also be converted to paths for subsequent editing as Illustrator objects.

Bitmapping and effect filters

You can incorporate bitmap images within Illustrator documents. External images can be placed within artworks and drawn objects rasterized (bitmapped) in situ. Special effects can be applied to such images using filters.

Outputting and exporting

You can output documents to desktop printers for proofing and printing. You can save them in an EPS file format for importing to DTP documents. You can also export artworks in a range of file formats for use in web pages, interactive presentations and multimedia projects. Furthermore, you can save files in Portable Document Format (PDF).

Conventions used in this book

Keystrokes in the main text are shown as icons, such as ⌘

When icons are separated by a + sign, as in ⌘ Option Shift + Delete , the modifier key(s) before the + sign should be held down together whilst the key after the + sign is pressed.

PC keyboards include an Alt instead of the Option key.

PC keyboards lack the Macintosh's ⌘ (Command) key. In all cases use the Control key instead.

Illustrator items, such as anchor points and direction lines, are often illustrated as they appear on screen.

Dialog boxes and palettes are generally illustrated as they appear on a Macintosh.

Other icons in this book are used in the following contexts.

● Single-step instructions and key points.

① Step-by-step instructions.

! Warnings and critical information.

▲ Helpful hints.

✚ Additional non-essential information.

2 | THE ILLUSTRATOR INTERFACE

Illustrator interface

This chapter is intended as a general reference to two key features of Illustrator, namely the Illustrator document window and the toolbox.

For those new to either the Macintosh or Windows, the final sub-section covers the standard controls used within each program.

The controls on each platform work in a similar manner although their appearance is subject to differing visual standards (see Figure 2.1).

If you are familiar with either system you can skip this later sub-section.

As far as the key Illustrator features are concerned, you may wish to just peruse the information and move on, referring back to it as and when necessary.

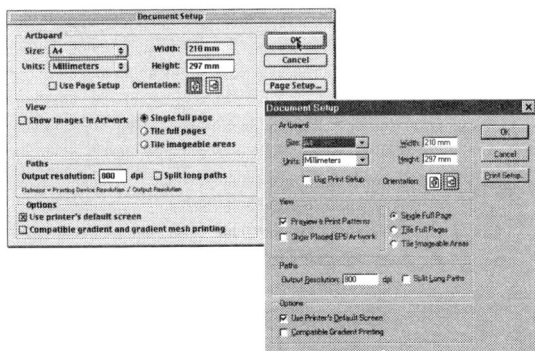

Figure 2.1 Windows control overlaying the Macintosh equivalent

Document window and toolbox

The document window

The document window (Figure 2.2) displays an open
Illustrator document.

Features include:

① title bar
② close box
③ zoom box
④ size box
⑤ artboard, with scratch
   area

⑥ scroll bars
⑦ rulers
⑧ ruler origin
⑨ view percent field
⑩ field showing current
   tool, date and time,
   free memory or
   number of undos

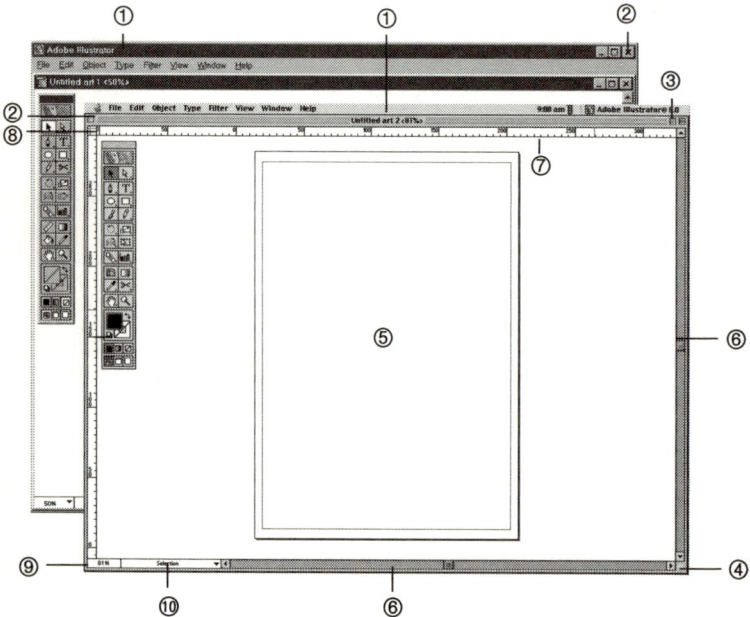

Figure 2.2 Macintosh document window overlayed over Windows version

The toolbox (Figure 2.3)

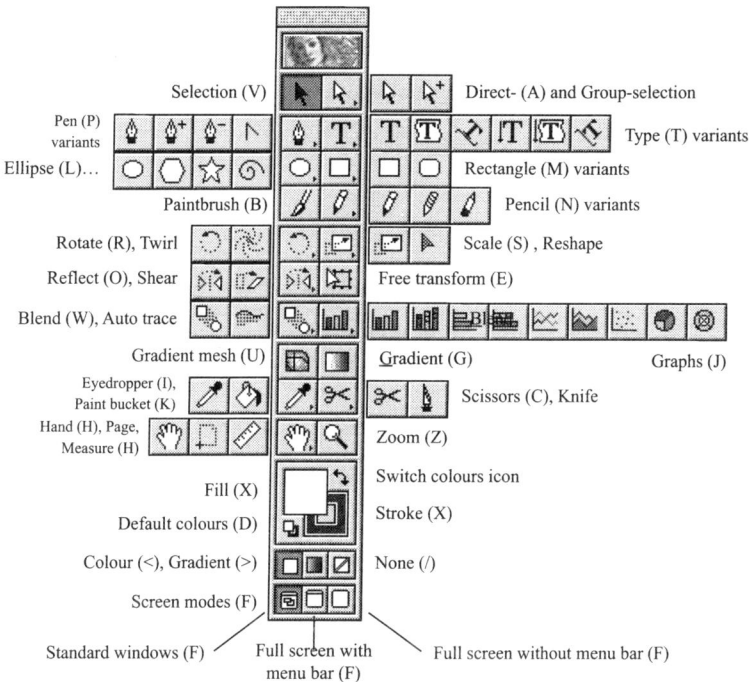

Selection (V)

Pen (P) variants

Ellipse (L)...

Paintbrush (B)

Rotate (R), Twirl

Reflect (O), Shear

Blend (W), Auto trace

Gradient mesh (U)

Eyedropper (I), Paint bucket (K)

Hand (H), Page, Measure (H)

Fill (X)

Default colours (D)

Colour (<), Gradient (>)

Screen modes (F)

Standard windows (F)

Full screen with menu bar (F)

Direct- (A) and Group-selection

Type (T) variants

Rectangle (M) variants

Pencil (N) variants

Scale (S) , Reshape

Free transform (E)

Gradient (G)

Graphs (J)

Scissors (C), Knife

Zoom (Z)

Switch colours icon

Stroke (X)

None (/)

Full screen without menu bar (F)

Figure 2.3 The toolbox

Selecting a tool

● Click once to select a tool. The pointer changes to the tool cursor. Click or click-drag on the image as appropriate.

▲ Press the Caps Lock key to turn icons into a crosshair pointer for precision working.

Select tools sharing the same location within the palette by either holding down the Alt key and clicking or click-dragging to the tool in the 'pop-up' menu. By click-dragging to select the small arrow you can tear off a miniature palette displaying all the variants together.

Press the Command (Control) key to temporarily access the current selection tool. Press the letters in parentheses for shortcuts to each tool.

Tools overview

Selection (V): for selecting whole objects

Direct-selection (A): for selecting points and segments

Group-selection: for selecting sub-groups

Pen (P): for drawing accurate paths

Pen variants: for editing paths

Type (T) variants: for typographic work

Ellipse (L) and Rectangle (M): for creating simple objects

Polygon, star, spiral: for creating simple objects

Paintbrush (B): for calligraphic work

Pencil (N): for freehand drawing

Pencil variants: for smoothing, editing and deleting paths

Rotate (R), Twirl, Reflect (O), Shear, Scale (S) and Free transform (E): for transforming objects and type

Reshape: for reshaping segments

Blend (W): for creating in-between objects and blends

Auto trace: for creating objects from bitmap images

Gradient mesh (U): for creating multiple gradients within objects

Gradient (G): for controlling gradients

Graph (J) variants: for creating graphs

Eyedropper (I) and Paint bucket (K): for selecting colours and filling areas

Scissors (C) and Knife: for cutting paths and shapes

Hand (H): for scrolling the image within the document window

Page: for altering the tiling area

Measure (H): for measuring distances

Zoom (Z): for altering the viewing scale

▲ Press the letters in parentheses for short-cuts to each tool.

Basic controls

Scroll bars

Every window within Illustrator has two scroll bars, one for vertical scrolling and one for horizontal scrolling. A grey scroll bar indicates more content beyond a window's borders; a clear bar indicates that all content is visible (see Figure 2.4).

Using the scroll bars

● Click the up, down, left or right scroll arrow.

Or:

● Click the vertical or horizontal scroll bar on either side of the scroll box, when it's grey.

Or:

● Drag the vertical or horizontal scroll box along its scroll bar.

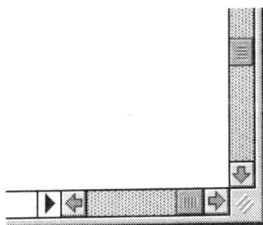

Figure 2.4 Vertical and horizontal scroll bars

Menus

Menus within Illustrator come in two types: pull-down menus and pop-up menus. The menus in the Illustrator menu bar are pull-down menus. Pop-up menus appear in palettes, dialog boxes or at the cursor, the latter being context-sensitive.

Selecting options from pull-down menus

● Point to the menu name, press to 'pull down' the menu, drag to the item you wish to choose so that it's highlighted and then release the mouse button.

Selecting options from pop-up menus

● Point to the visible menu item, press to 'pop up' the menu, drag to the item you wish to choose so that it's highlighted and then release the mouse button.

Selecting options from context-sensitive menus

● Hold down [Control], move the cursor over the object and press the mouse button. A menu appears (see Figure 2.5). Drag to the item you wish to choose so that it's highlighted and then release the mouse button.

▲ In Windows, there is no need to drag to the item you wish to choose in a a menu. Just press on the menu name or item and the full menu will be displayed. Then click on the item you wish to choose.

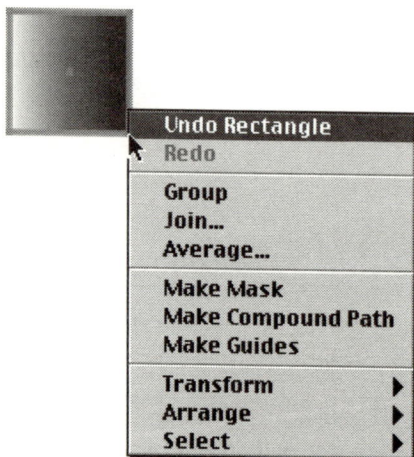

Figure 2.5 Example of a context-sensitive menu

Dialog boxes

In general, dialog boxes provide a means of specifying and applying artwork attributes. You can enter specifications into these boxes in a number of ways (see Figure 2.6). These boxes are modal so it's necessary to OK or cancel any settings before you can move on to other tasks.

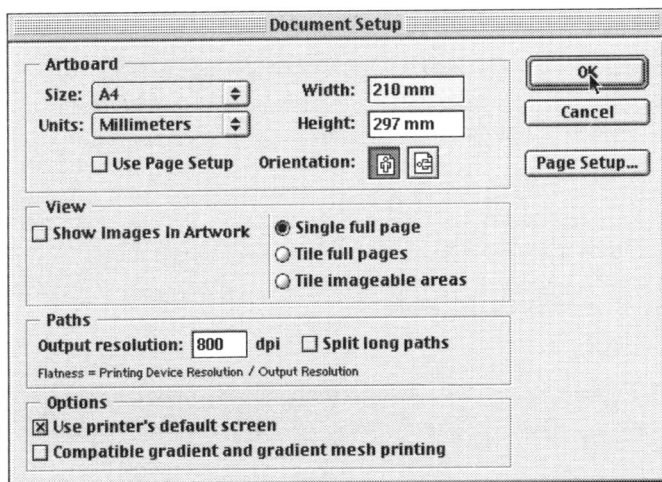

Figure 2.6 Dialog box with pop-up menus, fields and radio buttons

Entering new values in fields

① Double-click existing values (if not already highlighted).

② Type in new values.

Moving from field to field

● Press [Tab]

Checking boxes

Any number of boxes can be selected within a group of boxes.

● Click the box. An X or tick indicates that it's selected.

Clicking radio buttons

Only one button can be selected within a group of buttons.

● Click the button. An emboldened button indicates that it's selected.

Resetting specifications in dialog boxes

● Hold down [Option] to replace Cancel by Reset. Click Reset.

Applying specifications and closing box

● Click OK or press [Enter ↵].

Palettes

Palettes provide a further means of specifying and applying drawing attributes. Although their sets of controls are similar to those found in dialog boxes, they differ in that they can remain displayed at all times (see Figure 2.7).

Furthermore, palettes can be extended (see Figure 2.8) to show more options (in some cases) and nested together to save screen space.

Entering new values in fields

Either:

① Double-click existing values (if not already highlighted).

② Type in new values.

③ Press Enter.

Or:

① Click either of the small triangles to increase or decrease a value.

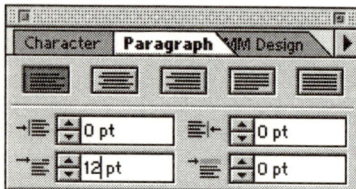

Figure 2.7 Entering a value by typing into a palette field

Selecting options from pop-up menus

● Point to the small triangle, press to 'pop up' the menu, drag to the item you wish to choose so that it's highlighted and then release the mouse button.

Moving from field to field

● Press ⌷Tab⌷

Extending palettes

● Choose Show Options from a palette's pop-menu.

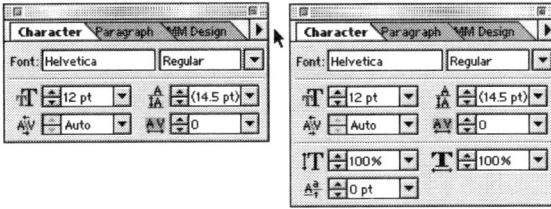

Figure 2.8 Example of palette in short and extended form

Nesting palettes

● Click-drag tab (named area) of palette to within area of palette in which you wish it to nest.

Separating palettes

● Click-drag tab of nested palette into blank area of document window.

Undoing work

You can correct mistakes in a number of ways in Illustrator.

Undoing a series of actions

● Choose Undo… in the Edit menu.

▲ You can set the number of undos in the Units and Undo set of preferences.

Redoing a series of actions

● Choose Redo… in the Edit menu.

Undoing unsaved work

You can undo unsaved work by reverting to the saved file on disk. If you use this method, it's important to save in a tactical way, anticipating the use of this command.

① Choose Revert in the File menu. An alert box saying 'Revert to a previously saved version of "…" ?' will be displayed.

② Click Revert to revert to saved. Click Cancel if you do not wish to revert.

Summary

Document window In addition
to the usual controls, the document
window can display key information, such as the number of undos
available.

Toolbox Tools can be selected by
just clicking on them or by using
keyboard shortcuts. They can also
be torn off as miniature palettes.

Basic controls Scroll bars,
menus, dialog boxes and palettes
work in a similar manner on PCs
and the Macintosh.

Dialog boxes Dialog boxes,
unlike palettes, are modal – you
need to close them down before
you can move on to the next task.

Palettes These movable controls
can be left open, nested together
and, in some cases extended to display additional controls.

Undoing and redoing work
Work can be undone and redone
within the Edit menu. Saved work
can also be reverted to if necessary.

3 CREATING AND SAVING DOCUMENTS

Creating documents

Starting a new document

Loading Illustrator

On the Macintosh

● Double-click on the Illustrator™ program icon within the Illustrator folder on your hard disk (see Figure 3.1).

! There is no need to double-click the icon on the Macintosh if it's greyed as this indicates that Illustrator is already running.

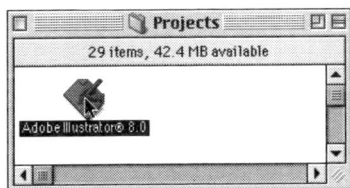

Figure 3.1 Opening a document in a folder

In Windows

● Choose Illustrator from the Programs sub-menu in the Start menu at the bottom left of the screen.

The Illustrator menu will be displayed. An Illustrator button will be added to the task bar.

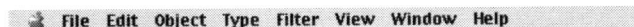

Macintosh menu bar

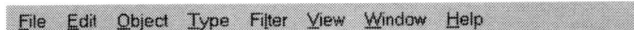

Windows menu bar

Altering the document setup

① Choose Document Setup... from the File menu. The Document Setup box will be displayed (see Figure 3.2).

! If the Illustrator menu is not showing, choose Illustrator from the Applications menu at the far right of the menu bar if on a Macintosh. On Windows, click the Illustrator button on the taskbar.

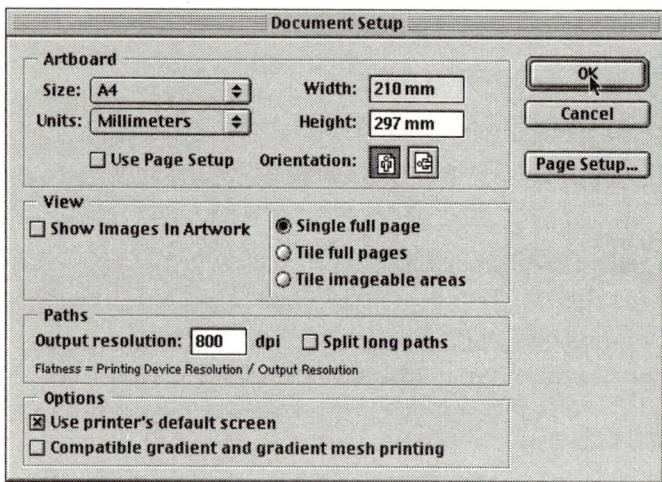

Figure 3.2 Altering a document's setup

Under Artboard:

② Either: choose an option in the Size pop-up menu or enter values in the Width and Height boxes.

Or: check or tick Use Page Setup box if you wish your artboard size to match the current page size in the Page Setup dialog box.

▲ When creating an illustration for importing into InDesign or other page layout programs, enter dimensions based on the final dimensions of the illustration.

For multimedia artwork, choose points in the units pop-up menu as they correspond to pixels.

Click the Page Setup button to access your printer's set of controls.

③ Click an orientation button.

Under View:

④ Click Single full page (see page 33).

Under Paths:

⑤ Enter a value of 800 in the Output Resolution field.

Under Options:

⑥ Check or tick Use printer's default screen.

⑦ Click OK.

▲ When you are entering values into fields in dialog boxes, it's best to double-click the existing values to highlight them, and then to enter the new value to overwrite them, either including the units of measure or not.

Saving documents

Saving a new document

Before you do any work in your new document, give it a name and save it to disk. You can save Illustrator documents in one of two ways: as a native Illustrator file or as an Illustrator EPS file. The former can't be imported into documents created by other page layout programs, whilst the latter can.

To avoid having two versions of the same artwork for printed work you can just save in Illustrator EPS if you wish. It retains as much information as a native Illustrator file, and with only one file to look after it simpifies file management.

If you are planning to output directly from Illustrator or to export your artwork as a bitmap, you need only to save in Illustrator format.

① Choose Save… from the File menu. The Save As directory dialog box will be displayed (see Figure 3.3).

② Enter a document name, overwriting the name 'Untitled Art 1'.

③ Select a drive and folder in which to save the file.

④ Select either Illustrator or Illustrator EPS in the Format pop-up menu.

⑤ Click Save. An EPS Format dialog box will be displayed (see Figure 3.4).

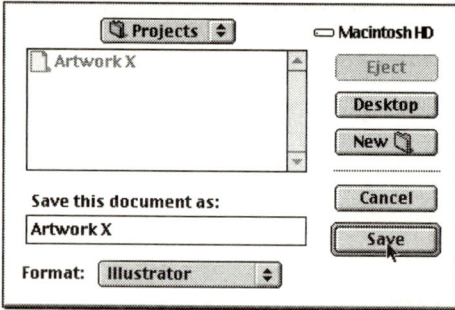

Figure 3.3 Saving a document in a folder called Projects

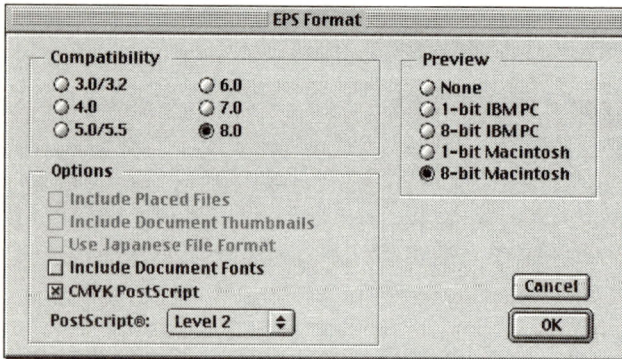

Figure 3.4 Saving a document in Illustrator EPS format

⑥ Under Compatibility select 8.0, or an older version of Illustrator if you have trouble outputting version 8 or if you plan to open the file using an earlier version of the program.

⑦ Under Preview (Illustrator EPS only) select either 8-bit IBM PC or Macintosh for colour and grayscale artworks and either 1-bit IBM PC or Macintosh for line artworks.

⑧ Click OK.

▲ You can also choose Portable Document Format (PDF) when saving a document (see page 177).

Resave every five minutes or so whilst you are working on a document, always using the Save command. The Save As dialog box will not be displayed on subsequent saves.

Although you can use up to 31 characters in a file name on a Macintosh and even more on Windows, it's best to restrict yourself to around 20 so that names show in full and without being compressed within directory dialog boxes.

✦ On Windows, Illustrator files have a .ai extension and Illustrator EPS files have a .eps extension.

Opening and closing documents

Opening an existing document

Either:

① Choose Open... from the Illustrator's File menu. The Open directory dialog box will be displayed (see Figure 3.5).

Macintosh menu bar

Windows menu bar

If the Illustrator menu is not showing on the Macintosh, choose Illustrator from the Applications menu at the far right of the menu bar. On Windows, click the Illustrator button on the taskbar. If neither is present, launch Illustrator. See Loading Illustrator (page 15).

② Use the directory dialog box controls to locate your document.

③ Click Open. The document window will be displayed.

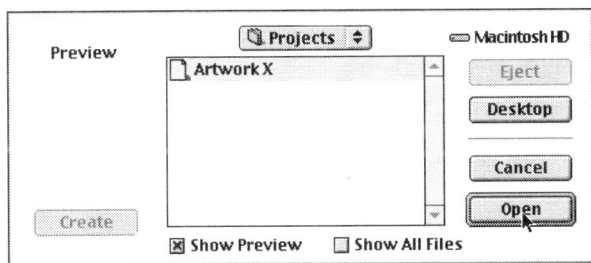

Figure 3.5 Opening a saved document

Or:

● Double-click on its document icon within its folder window.
  The document window will be displayed.

▲ On the Macintosh, folders are accessed from icons on the desktop. On
  Windows, folders are accessed via My Computer.

✚ If Illustrator has not already been running it will now be loaded. Its title
  and menu bar will soon be displayed.

Creating a copy of a document

Often you will wish to retain a version of a document in its current state
and move on to a copy of a document instead. Doing this gives you the
opportunity to revert back to an earlier version should your later work
turn out to be unsound.

① Choose Save from the File menu if you wish the closing
  document to contain your latest work. Otherwise omit this
  step.

② Choose Save As... from the File menu. The Save As
  directory dialog box will be displayed (see Figure 3.6).

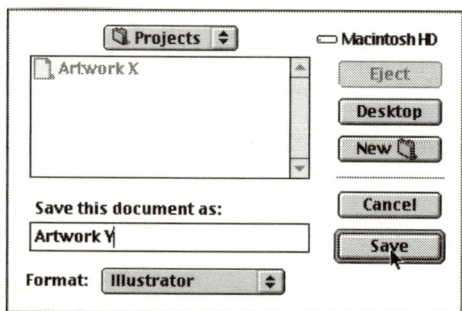

Figure 3.6 Saving a copy of a document in a folder called Projects

③ Enter a different document name, overwriting its existing
  name.

④ Select a drive and folder in which to save the file.

⑤ Choose Illustrator or Illustrator EPS from the Format pop-
  up menu.

⑥ Click Save to save the document. Click Cancel if you wish to abort the routine.

Closing documents

① Click the Close box at the top left of the document window on the Macintosh. On Windows, click the close icon at the top right of the document window.

② An alert box saying 'Save changes to the Adobe Illustrator document "…" before closing?' will be displayed.

③ Click Yes to save the document. Click No if you do not wish to save a new document or recent work.

Quitting Illustrator

① Choose Quit from the File menu.

② An alert box saying 'Save changes to the Adobe Illustrator document "…" before closing?' will be displayed if your document is still open and recent work has not been saved.

③ Click Yes to save the document. Click No if you do not wish to save a new document or recent work.

Summary

Starting documents All new documents are started by choosing Document from the New… sub-menu in Illustrator's File menu.

Opening documents Open a saved document within its folder window or by choosing Open… from Illustrator's File menu.

Saving documents Save a newly created document by choosing Save… from Illustrator's File menu.

Naming documents Always give a new document a descriptive name, preferably no longer than 20 characters.

Retaining document versions Move on to a copy of a document by choosing Save As… from Illustrator's File menu.

4 | VIEWING AND MARKING UP THE ARTBOARD

Working with the artboard

Viewing at different scales

Artwork can be viewed within Illustrator in a number of scales ranging from 3.13% to 6400%. When you view at actual size (100% in the document window title bar), your work is shown roughly life size on screen. The scale ratio you choose does not directly affect your artwork so view at any scale which allows you to perform a given task with ease.

The viewing scale can be altered by using the View menu, by using the Zoom tool (with or without a modifier key), by pressing keystrokes, by entering a percentage (%) value in the scale field in the document window or by means of the Navigator palette.

Using the tool box icons and keystrokes

You can fit artwork to the document window or view at 100% scale by simply double-clicking the Hand or Zoom tool icons.

- ● Double-click the Hand tool to fit artwork to window.

- ● Double-click the Zoom tool to view artwork at actual size.

▲ Press Command (Control)–0 to fit window and Command (Control)–1 to view at actual size if a dialog box is open.

Using the Zoom tool and keystrokes

You can scale artwork at any size using the Zoom tool or, better still, temporarily accessing the tool using keystrokes. The latter way saves time as it does not require you to 'drop' the tool you are working with.

① Select the Zoom tool (or hold down ⌘ + [Space]) and click within your artwork (or click-drag diagonally across part of it) to increase the viewing scale.

② Hold down [Option] at the same time (or hold down [⌘][Option] + [Space]) and click within your artwork to reduce the viewing scale.

③ Reselect another tool to deselect the Zoom tool (if selected from the toolbox).

! The keyboard shortcut allows you to alter the viewing scale when a dialog box is open.

Using the Navigator palette

You can also scale artwork by means of the Navigator palette.

Choose Show Navigator in the Window menu. The Navigator palette will be displayed (see Figure 4.1).

● Click the Zoom in and Zoom out icons or click-drag the Zoom Slider to alter the scale.

Or:

● Enter a percentage (%) value in the bottom left scale field.

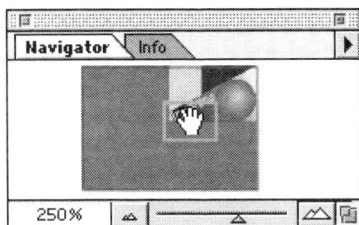

Figure 4.1 Click-dragging the red rectangle in the Navigator palette

Moving around the artboard

You can move around the artboard using the scroll bars, the Hand tool and by means of the Navigator palette.

Moving an artwork within the document window

● Use the scroll bars.

Or:

● Select the Hand tool (or hold down Space bar) and click-drag within the document window.

Or:

● Click-drag the red rectangle within the Preview Area in the Navigator palette (see Figure 4.1).

Saving views

You may wish to regularly switch between views of your artwork. If this is the case you can save individual views and call them up as menu commands. Doing this will save you a lot of repetitive scaling and scrolling work.

① Scale and scroll to establish an optimum view of your artwork within the document window.

② Choose New View... in the View menu. The New View dialog box will be displayed.

③ Enter a name in the Name field.

④ Click OK. The saved view will be listed at the bottom of the View menu with its keyboard shortcut. Choose the command whenever you wish to revert to that view.

Viewing modes

You can preview artwork with strokes, fills and bitmap images fully rendered and with unstroked and unfilled paths made invisible (see Figure 4.2).

● Choose Preview from the View menu. The word Artwork will take the place of the word Preview in the menu.

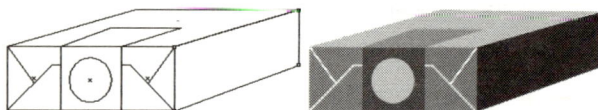

Figure 4.2 The same drawing in Artwork mode (left) and Preview mode (right)

Alternatively you can view all artwork solely as path structures including those objects that lack strokes and fills. The absence of such attributes facilitates path editing whilst the fact that all objects are displayed at once allows you to easily identify those that are unwanted. A further advantage of working in this view is that it speeds screen redrawing.

● Choose Artwork from the View menu. The word Preview will take the place of the word Artwork in the menu.

Furthermore you can work in Preview Selection mode. In this mode object paths appear as in Artwork mode unless they are selected in which case they are previewed. This helps in identifying and selecting objects in close proximity to one another.

● Choose Preview Selection from the View menu (to tick the command).

Hiding/displaying interface items

Windows, menu bars and palettes can be visible or hidden when you work.

Showing and hiding windows and menu bars

● Click one of the screen modes at the bottom of the toolbox (see Figure 4.3).

Figure 4.3 Screen mode buttons

Showing and hiding all palettes

● Press Tab

Showing individual palettes

● Choose a palette from the Window menu.

Hiding/displaying non-printing items

Showing guides

● Choose Show Guides from the View menu. If the guides are already showing, the word 'Hide' will precede the command.

Showing the grid

● Choose Show Grid from the View menu. If the grid is already showing, the word 'Hide' will precede the command.

Showing selection borders

Individual paths can be shown when multiple objects are selected.

● Choose Show Edges from the View menu. If edges are already visible, the word 'Hide' will precede the command.

Showing bounding boxes

Bounding boxes allow you to scale, move and copy multiple objects solely through the use of the Selection tool.

① Choose General… from the Preferences sub-menu in the File menu. The General set of preferences will be displayed.

② Check or tick Use bounding box.

③ Click OK.

Setting up the rulers

Rulers can be displayed at the top and left side of Illustrator's document window. Their increment varies according to the current view scale so you'll see more tick marks representing finer amounts the closer you view. Dotted lines in each ruler constantly track the position of the cursor to assist you in object positioning.

Showing and hiding rulers

● Choose Show Rulers in the View menu. If the rulers are already showing, the word 'Hide' will precede the command.

Altering the ruler units

The rulers can be calibrated in any one of five measurements units.

① Choose Units & Undo… in the Preferences sub-menu in the File menu. The Units Preferences dialog box will be displayed.

② Choose an option in the Units pop-up menu (see Figure 4.4).

③ Click OK.

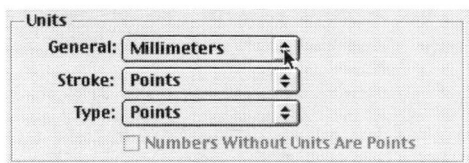

Figure 4.4 The Units preferences

▲ For multimedia artwork, choose points in the General pop-up menu as they correspond to pixels.

Moving the ruler zero points

The rulers normally measure from the bottom and left edges of the artboard. If you are working within a defined area of the artboard you can move the zero point to the bottom left corner of this area or to any other place of your choosing.

① Click-drag from the small square at the junction of the rulers to a position within the artboard.

② Release the mouse button. The zero points will have moved accordingly (see Figure 4.5).

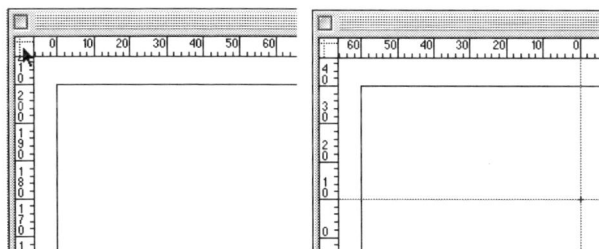

Figure 4.5 Moving the ruler zero point

▲ Double-click within the same square from which you have just dragged to return the zero point to its original position.

Working with ruler guides

These non-printing construction lines are used for defining the principal areas and alignments within an artwork. They are a key aid to accurate object placement, especially when used in conjunction with Snap to

Point. Snap to Point ensures the cursor is attracted to guides when it comes within a two pixel distance from them.

Ruler guides are dragged out from the rulers and are thus vertical and horizontal in orientation. Unusually for such guide types, they can be released to become ordinary Illustrator paths. Once released, if you do not wish them to become part of your artwork content, ensure they are either deleted or made into guides again (see Working with object guides later in this chapter).

Setting the appearance of guides

① Choose Guides and Grid... from the Preferences sub-menu in the File menu. The Guides and Grid set of preferences will be displayed.

② Under Guides, choose an option from the Colour pop-up menu. The colour swatch will alter to reflect the chosen colour.

③ Under Guides, choose Lines or Dots from the Style pop-up menu.

④ Click OK.

Working with ruler guides

Adding a ruler guide

● Click-drag from somewhere in the middle of either ruler to a position within the artboard. Release the mouse button when you have reached the desired location (see Figure 4.6).

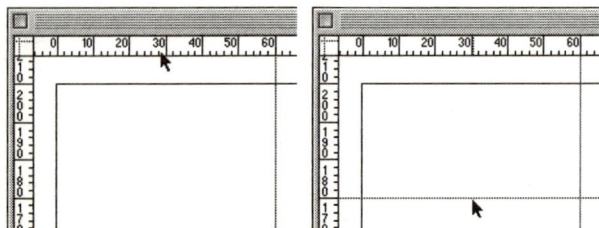

Figure 4.6 Creating ruler guides

▲ Choose a viewing scale above 200% to position guides with greater accuracy.

Moving a ruler guide

① Choose Lock Guides from the View menu (to untick the command). This unlocks all guides.

② Click-drag any guide you wish to move.

③ Choose Lock Guides again from the View menu (to tick the command). This relocks all guides.

Removing a ruler guide

① Choose Lock Guides from the View menu (to untick the command). This unlocks all guides.

② Click on the guide you wish to remove.

③ Press Delete.

④ Choose Lock Guides again from the View menu (to retick the command). This relocks all guides.

Locking all guides

● Choose Lock Guides from the View menu.

Snapping objects to guides

● Choose Snap to Point from the View menu (to tick the command).

Working with grids

Unlike ruler guides, grids provide repeated alignment points right across the artboard. Like graph paper they provide a high level of positional accuracy enabling technical drawings in various projections to be easily constructed (see Figure 4.7).

Grids can also give rigour and order to non-technical illustrations and graphic motifs and provide a way of establishing visual consistency between artworks.

You can choose a grid's size and appearance to suit your needs and you can snap points to the nearest grid intersection by enabling Snap to Grid.

Setting up a grid

① Choose Guides and Grid… from the Preferences sub-menu in the File menu. The Guides and Grid set of preferences will be displayed.

② Under Grid, choose an option from the Colour pop-up menu. The colour swatch will alter to reflect the chosen colour.

③ Under Grid, choose Lines or Dots from the Style pop-up menu.

④ Enter a value in the Gridline every field.

⑤ Enter a value in the Subdivisions field.

⑥ Check or tick Grid in Back if you wish the grid to run behind your drawing.

⑦ Click OK.

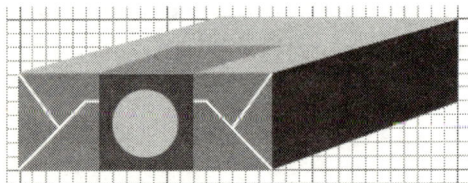

Figure 4.7 Drawing based on grid

Snapping points to grid intersections

● Choose Snap to Grid from the View menu (to tick the command).

Working with object guides

I've described how you work with ruler guides and grids. Illustrator offers a further type of guide which can be created from objects you create yourselves. The objects can be the shape of an item, such as a light bulb, or can be intersecting parallel lines making up an axonometric grid. But mostly they will be created from rectangular objects defining the dimensions of your work.

Since they can be in any configuration you wish they are particularly flexible positional tools.

Creating object guides

● Select an object and choose Make Guides from the View menu.

▲ Remove object guides in the same way as ruler guides.

Releasing object guides

① Choose Lock Guides from the View menu (to untick the command). This unlocks all guides.

② Select an object and choose Release Guides from the View menu.

Snapping to guides

● Choose Snap to Points from the View menu (to tick the command).

Working with temporary guides

You can also snap objects to temporary guides called Smart Guides. These guides help you to create, align, edit and transform objects in relation to other objects irrespective of where they are on the artboard or whether they are locked.

Working with such guides can be a bit tricky at first as the technique appears a bit volatile. When Smart Guides is enabled, the cursor creates temporary guides when positioned close to objects, page boundaries and ruler/object guides. By moving the cursor relative to these items a position can be established for the aligning object (see Chapter 8 on the use of Smart Guides).

The angle of the temporary guides can be selected from those chosen in the Smart Guide preferences.

Enabling Smart Guides

● Choose Smart Guides from the View menu (to tick the command).

! Snap to Grid needs to be turned off for Smart Guides to operate.

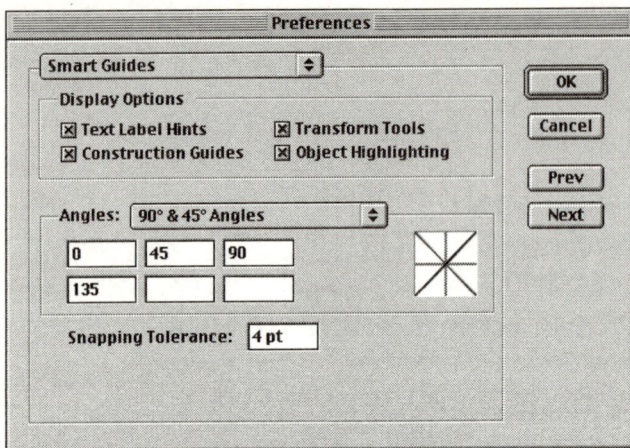

Figure 4.8 Working with Smart Guides

Setting up Smart Guides

① Choose Smart Guides... from the Preferences sub-menu in the File menu. The Smart Guides preferences dialog box will be displayed (see Figure 4.8).

② Under Display Options, check or tick Text Label Hints (to help with the cursor positioning), Construction Guides (to be able to align to these), Transform Tools (to help with tranformations) and Object Highlighting (to highlight objects as you drag the cursor over them).

③ Choose an option in the Angles pop-up menu. If you wish to customize a set of angles enter values in the Angle fields.

④ Enter a figure in the Snapping tolerance field.

⑤ Click OK.

Viewing printing areas

If you are outputting your Illustrator artwork directly to a desktop printer, its paper size and margins effectively limit the area in which you can work. To ensure you don't work outside this area, Illustrator uses a feature called page tiling.

Tiling defines the area of the artboard which falls within the printing area of your chosen printer and is determined by the paper size and orientation selected in the Page Setup dialog box.

Tiling does not affect the properties of your illustration in any way. It may not even be of relevance to you. If you are creating an artwork for importing into InDesign or QuarkXPress, its position is determined by page layout factors unconnected with Illustrator. In such cases, you can hide the tiling so it does not clutter your view of the artboard.

Altering the page tiling

① Select Document Setup... from the File menu. The Document Setup dialog box will be displayed.

② Under View, select one of three options (see Figure 4.9):

Single full page: choose this option for single page content you wish to *finally* output on your chosen digital printing device.

Tile full pages: choose this option for double-page spread content you wish to *finally* output on your chosen digital printing device.

Tile imageable areas: this option indicates how a piece of artwork larger than your printer's page size is tiled when output. It excludes margins as the tiling does not represent page areas in your design. Choose it for large-scale content you wish to *finally* output on a large format printing device.

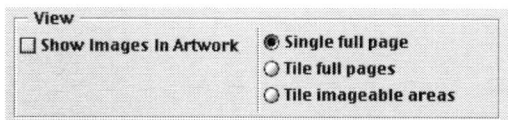

Figure 4.9 The tiling options in the Document Setup dialog box

Showing page tiling

● Choose Show Page Tiling from the View menu. If the page tiling is already showing, the word 'Hide' will precede the command.

Positioning the tiling within the artboard

● Select the Page tool and click-drag on artwork area.

Summary

Viewing View at any scale which allows you to perform a given task with ease.

Moving around Move around the artboard using the scroll bars, Hand tool or Navigation palette.

Ruler guides Use ruler guides to establish key alignments within your artwork.

Grids Use grids to give rigour and order to technical drawings.

Object guides Let the shape of objects themselves act as artwork guides.

Snap to points Enable Snap to points to snap objects, including points, to other points and guides.

Page tiling Use tiling to indicate printing areas on your desktop printer.

5 | DRAWING LINES AND SHAPES

Basic concepts

All drawing in Illustrator is constructed from lines called paths. It is the way you work with paths that gives form and meaning to your artwork.

Paths are made up of segments with connecting parts called anchor points (see Figure 5.1). There are essentially two types of anchor point: corner points and smooth points.

Whilst smooth points always have direction lines associated with them ensuring that curves flow in and out of them smoothly, corner points have direction lines associated with them only if a connecting segment is curved. Otherwise they lack direction lines.

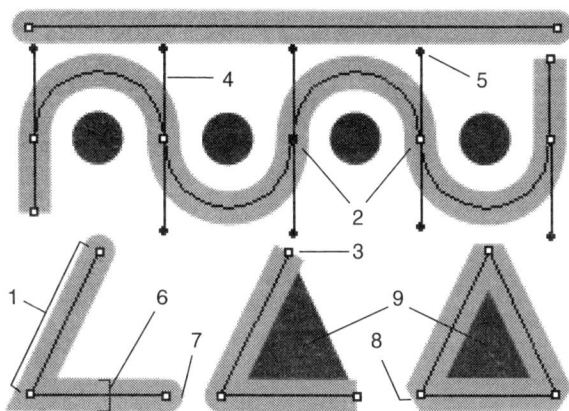

Figure 5.1 Path components: segment (1), point (2), end point (3), direction line (4), direction point (5), stroke (6), end cap (7), join (8), fill (9)

Illustrator paths can be open-ended, as lines, or closed, as outlines. Either way they can be given strokes – widths, colours and other attributes – and fills – colours, gradients and such like.

Paths are created by:

- The Pencil tool. Paths are automatically created along a line tracked by the mouse.

- The Paintbrush tool. Closed paths of varying width are automatically created along a line tracked by the mouse.

- The Pen tool. Paths are created by plotting points and segments.

- The Auto trace tool. The program automatically traces the edges of placed images to plot points and segments for you.

Simple shapes are created by:

- The Rectangle, Rounded rectangle, Ellipse, Polygon, Star and Spiral tools.

Drawing for the first time

You can either draw in Artwork mode, where strokes and fills are not rendered, or you can draw in Preview mode.

If you decide to draw in Preview mode and you are planning to just draw lines, set the fill colour to None and the stroke colour to 100% black. If you are planning to draw shapes, set the fill colour to 35% black and the stroke colour to 100% black (see Chapter 6).

Finally set the stroke width to 1 pt or more (see Applying strokes later in this chapter). The fill and stroke boxes should appear as in Figure 5.2.

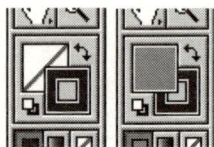

Figure 5.2 How the fill and stroke boxes in the Toolbox should appear for lines (left) and for shapes (right). These settings are recommended when drawing for the first time

Drawing freely

Drawing with the Pencil

The Pencil tool enables drawings to be made spontaneously using a mouse or graphics tablet (see Figure 5.3). It also enables you to edit paths created by other tools, not just those drawn by the Pencil (see Reshaping paths later in this chapter).

● With the Pencil tool active, click-drag on the artboard as if you are using a pencil on a sheet of paper.

Illustrator automatically converts the movement of the cursor into points and segments of a path.

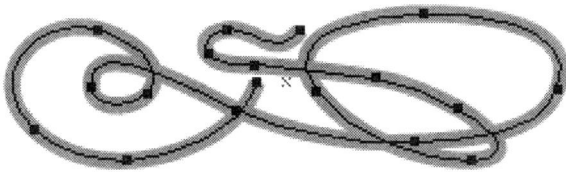

Figure 5.3 Drawing freely with the Pencil

Extending a previously completed path

Either

● Position Pencil tool over end point and click-drag.

Or:

● Position Pen tool over end point and click-drag (see later in this chapter on the use of this tool).

Smoothing out a path

① Select path.

② With the Smooth tool active, click-drag along the line of path you wish to smooth out (see Figure 5.4).

Illustrator may reduce the number of anchor points in the process of smoothing.

Figure 5.4 The Smooth and Eraser tools

Erasing a path

① Select path.

② With the Erase tool active, click-drag along the line of path you wish to erase (not across the path).

Illustrator will add anchor points to the ends of new paths.

Closing a path

● Whilst still drawing, press ⌷Option⌷. If the cursor is positioned other than at the start of the path, a straight segment will close the path.

Painting with the Paintbrush

The Paintbrush enables calligraphic shapes to be drawn spontaneously using a mouse or graphics tablet. Unlike the Pencil, the Paintbrush automatically creates closed paths with an angled stress (see Figure 5.5).

● With the Paintbrush tool active, click-drag on the artboard as if you are using a brush on a sheet of paper.

Figure 5.5 Drawing calligraphically with the Paintbrush

▲ Double-click the Pencil or Paintbrush icon in the toolbox to access their preferences. Low Smoothness and Fidelity settings create more faithful strokes and curves. High Smoothness and Fidelity settings tend to create smoother strokes and curves (see Figure 5.6).

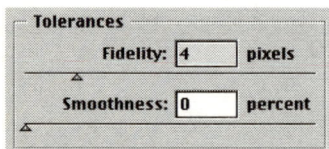

Figure 5.6 Pencil and Paintbrush tool tolerances

Creating simple geometric shapes

You can create simple geometric shapes within Illustrator without having to plot out their points yourself (see Figures 5.7 and 5.9). And since they are constructed from the same components as other paths the shapes can be modified at will.

Whether you are good at drawing or not, it's wise to use the basic shape tools to create such forms as you can be sure they have been accurately constructed.

If you are drawing in Preview mode, when using these tools for the first time set the fill colour to 35% black and the stroke colour to 100% black. Then set the stroke width to 1 pt or more.

Creating rectangles and ellipses

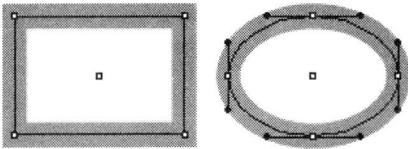

Figure 5.7 Rectangle and ellipse, the latter shown with segments selected

① With the Rectangle, Rounded rectangle or Ellipse tool active

Either:

② Move the mouse (without pressing the button) over to the artboard. The pointer turns into a cross hair.

③ Click-drag diagonally upwards or downwards.

④ Release the mouse button.

Or:

② Click on the artboard. A dialog box will be displayed (see Figure 5.8).

③ Enter values in the Height and Width fields. In the case of the Rounded rectangle enter a value in the Corner Radius field.

④ Click OK.

▲ Hold down the Shift key when click-dragging to create squares and circles. Hold down the Alt key to draw from a centre point.

Once a rectangle or ellipse has been created you can alter its dimensions within the Transform palette (see page 104).

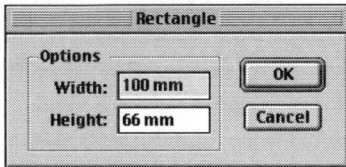

Figure 5.8 Entering dimensions in the Rectangle dialog box

Creating spirals, stars and polygons

Figure 5.9 Stars, spiral and polygons

① With the Polygon, Spiral or Star tool active.

Either:

② Move the mouse (without pressing the button) over to the artboard. The pointer turns into a cross hair.

③ Click-drag diagonally upwards or downwards.

④ Release the mouse button.

Or:

② Press the Alt key and click on the artboard. A dialog box will be displayed (see Figure 5.10).

④ Specify attributes as appropriate.

In the case of the Spiral, enter the distance from the centre of the polygon to the outermost point in the Radius field, the amount of wind in the Decay field and the number of segments (based on four to a full wind) in the Segments field. Under Style select either Counterclockwise or Clockwise.

In the case of the Star, enter the distance from the centre of the polygon to the innermost point in the first Radius field and to the outermost point in the second Radius field. Enter the number of sides to the star in the Points field.

In the case of the Polygon, enter the distance from the centre of the polygon to the end points in the Radius field and the number of sides in the Sides field.

⑤ Click OK.

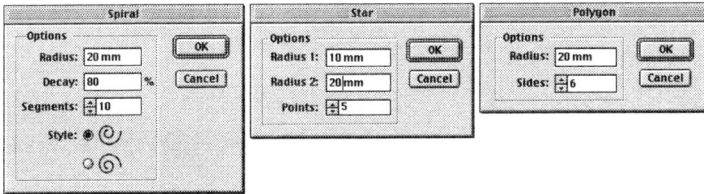

Figure 5.10 The Spiral, Star and Polygon dialog boxes

Drawing with the Pen tool

The Pen tool (see Figure 5.11) allows you to create straight lines and curves with utmost precision. It's the most flexible and powerful of the drawing tools in Illustrator and the one you will use most to create lines and shapes with artworks.

Figure 5.11 The Pen tool

You draw with the Pen tool by clicking or click-dragging with the mouse. Clicking the mouse creates corner points and click-dragging creates smooth points, complete with direction lines (see Figure 5.12).

Figure 5.12 Clicking creates straight line segments (left) whilst click-dragging creates curved segments (right)

Using the tool for the first time

When using the Pen tool for the first time it's probably best to work in Preview mode with the fill colour set to None and the stroke colour set to 100% black. The stroke width should be 1 pt or more.

Drawing straight lines

① With the Pen tool selected, position the tip of the pen cursor where you wish the straight line to begin. (A small multiplication sign will appear beside the pen cursor to denote it's ready to create the first point.) Click to create the first anchor point. The anchor point remains selected (appears solid) until the next point is created.

② Click again where you wish the first straight line segment to end.

③ Click again at the end of each straight line segment.

Completing paths

Use this method to close a path.

● Click the starting anchor point. (A small circle will appear beside the pen cursor to denote it's over the first point.)

Use either of these methods to complete an open-ended path so you can start a new path:

● Press ⌘ and click on blank area of artboard.

● Choose Deselect All from the Edit menu or press ⌘ Shift + A.

● Select another tool.

Redoing an anchor point

If you have made a mistake when creating an anchor point you can rectify the situation by one of the following actions.

Either:

● Choose Undo… in the Edit menu and then create a new anchor point.

Or:

● press ⌈Delete⌋, click or click-drag the previous anchor point depending on whether it is a corner point or a smooth point. Then create a new anchor point.

Drawing curved paths

To define curved segments, anchor points need to have direction lines – Bézier handles – associated with them.

When you click-drag with the Pen tool, these lines are automatically in alignment and it is this alignment that ensures that curved segments on either side of the point flow smoothly into one another. At path angles – where curved segments spring out in different directions – it's necessary to have non-aligned direction lines or a single direction line. This is achieved by manipulating existing direction lines, by adding and manipulating new direction lines or by deleting direction lines.

The length and orientation of direction lines

The position of anchor points and the length and orientation of their direction lines determines the size and shape of curved segments. The direction lines are always tangential to – touching – the curve at the anchor points. The angle – orientation – of a direction line relative to a segment determines the slope of the curve whilst the length of a direction line determines the depth of the curve. (See Where to locate anchor points later in this chapter)

Adjusting direction lines

Segments of wavy paths and of some single curves are connected by smooth points. Non-continuous curves, i.e. curves that spring from corners, are connected by corner points. When you move a direction line on a smooth point, the curves on both sides of the points are adjusted, whereas when you move a direction line on a corner point, only the curve on the same side of the point is adjusted.

▲ Drawing curved paths on a blank area of artboard is difficult even for an experienced draughtsman as one is having to invent the line of a path as one plots it. Practice using the tool by plotting around the edge of a scanned image placed specially for this purpose. It's much easier to draw this way as you are able to focus your mind solely on the use of the tool rather than having to invent shapes.

Drawing approaches

As the Pen tool is difficult to use at the best of times, some people plot out their paths just by using corner points and then add direction lines to some of these points on path completion.

However it's better if you can get used to drawing using the correct points from the start and to restrict any editing work to fine-tuning. Most people work this way and once they get to know the ropes they fine tune as they go along rather than wait till a path is completed, using the modifier keys to temporarily access the necessary tools.

Drawing curves

Drawing undulating curves

① With the Pen tool selected, position the tip of the pen cursor where you wish the wavy line to begin. (A small multiplication sign will appear beside the pen cursor to denote it's ready to create the first point.) Click-drag in a forward direction (tangentially to the first curve) to create the first anchor point. The anchor point remains selected (appears solid) until the next point is created.

② Click-drag again in the same manner at a position where you wish the curve to change direction.

③ Repeat step 2 for each change of curve direction (see Figure 5.13).

Figure 5.13 Smooth points where curves change direction. All segments have been selected for clarity

▲ When you create a smooth point adjust the length and orientation of its leading direction handle (the one the Pen tool is pulling out of the point) to create a trailing segment of the desired curvature. If this leading direction line is to be left in place (in the context of wavy lines it will be) it may need to be shortened if the following curved segment is short, otherwise the segment will be 'cockled'.

Curving in or out of a straight

By aligning the direction lines of a smooth point with a trailing straight line segment a smooth transition is ensured between the two segments (see Figure 5.14).

Figure 5.14 Aligning direction lines with a trailing straight line segment. All segments have been selected for clarity

Curving in and out of an angle

You draw curved segments from angles by either deleting the leading direction line of a smooth point or by adjusting its angle. Either way you need to select the Direct-selection tool before using the Pen tool.

By deleting the leading direction line of a smooth point, you can spring a new curved segment from the point.

    ① Click on the smooth point you have just created. (A small carat will appear beside the pen cursor to denote it's over the point.) Its leading direction line will be deleted (see Figure 5.15).

    ② Click-drag to create the next smooth point.

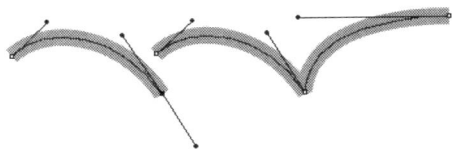

Figure 5.15 Newly created smooth point with two direction lines (left) and with its leading direction line removed and the next smooth point plotted (right). All segments have been selected for clarity

Rather than deleting the leading direction line you can adjust its angle to create a new curved segment of greater subtlety. At the same time as doing this you can also re-angle the trailing direction line to adjust the curve of the previous segment (see Figure 5.16).

① Hold down ⌘ and then Option once you have created a
smooth point. When both keys are held down, the cursor
appears like the Group-selection icon.

② Click-drag either direction point (the end point of either
direction line).

Figure 5.16 Newly created smooth point with two direction lines (left) and with its
leading direction line re-angled and the next smooth point plotted (right). All
segments have been selected for clarity

Curving abruptly out of a straight

By adding a leading direction to a corner point, you can spring a curved
segment out from the point.

Figure 5.17 Corner point at end of straight segment (left) and with leading
direction line added and the next smooth point plotted (right). All segments have
been selected for clarity

① Hold down Option and click-drag from corner point you have
just created. (A small carat will appear beside the pen cursor
to denote it's over the point.) A direction line will be drawn
out of the point (see Figure 5.17). Orientate the direction
line to suit the curved segment yet to be drawn.

② Click-drag to created the next smooth point.

! The first direction line you add to a corner point will always be leading
(controlling the following segment). The second direction line will be
trailing (controlling the previous segment).

Points to bear in mind

When you are drawing paths bear the following in mind:

- View at a scale that allows you to follow a path accurately on-screen.
- Create only as many anchor points as you need to draw a path, especially when drawing curved segments.
- Keep direction lines reasonably short. They should generally be between one-quarter and one-half of the length of the segments they are defining.
- Avoid creating anchor points over direction points (the ends of direction lines), as this leads to confusion.

Since all curves are defined by direction lines, they are more likely to be smooth if the number of points are kept to the minimum. Every direction line influences a segment whether you like it or not so don't use any more than you need.

Constraining points and direction lines

You can constrain direction lines and path angles to 45 degree increments.

Constraining anchor points

- Hold down [Shift] and click when creating corner points.

Constraining direction lines

- Hold down [Shift] and click-drag when creating smooth points.

Moving anchor points as you create them

Use this key-stroke to create an anchor point you can immediately move.

① Hold down [Space] after you have created a point but before you have released the mouse button, whilst creating a new point.

② Drag point to reposition it before releasing [Space].

Where to locate anchor points

The key to drawing with the tool is to know where to create points and how to configure their direction lines.

- Locate corner points:

  Where straight segments meet at a corner.

  Where curved segments spring out of straight segments.

  Where straight segments flow into curved segments.

  Where curved segments spring off in different directions.

- Locate smooth points:

  Where curved segments change direction.

  At the peaks and troughs of curves. The need for points at such locations depends on the complexity of the curve to be drawn.

Creating a drawing using the Pen tool

Here we create a drawing of a support for a table (see Figure 5.18). There are 12 steps to this exercise involving 12 anchor points.

① Click to create corner point. Release mouse.

② Click to create corner point. Release mouse. Hold down Alt and click-drag at 4 o'clock direction to pull out its leading direction line. Release mouse and Alt key.

③ Click-drag at 3–4 o'clock direction to create smooth point. Release mouse.

④ Click-drag at 3 o'clock direction to create smooth point. Release mouse. Hold down Alt and click on point to remove its leading direction line.

⑤ Click-drag at 7 o'clock direction to create smooth point. Hold down Alt and click on point to remove its leading direction line.

⑥ Hold down Shift and click to create corner point level with point 5. Release mouse and Shift key. Hold down Alt and click-drag at 5 o'clock direction to pull out its leading direction line. Release mouse and Alt key.

⑦ Click-drag at 4 o'clock direction to create smooth point. Release mouse. Hold down Alt and click on point to remove leading direction line.

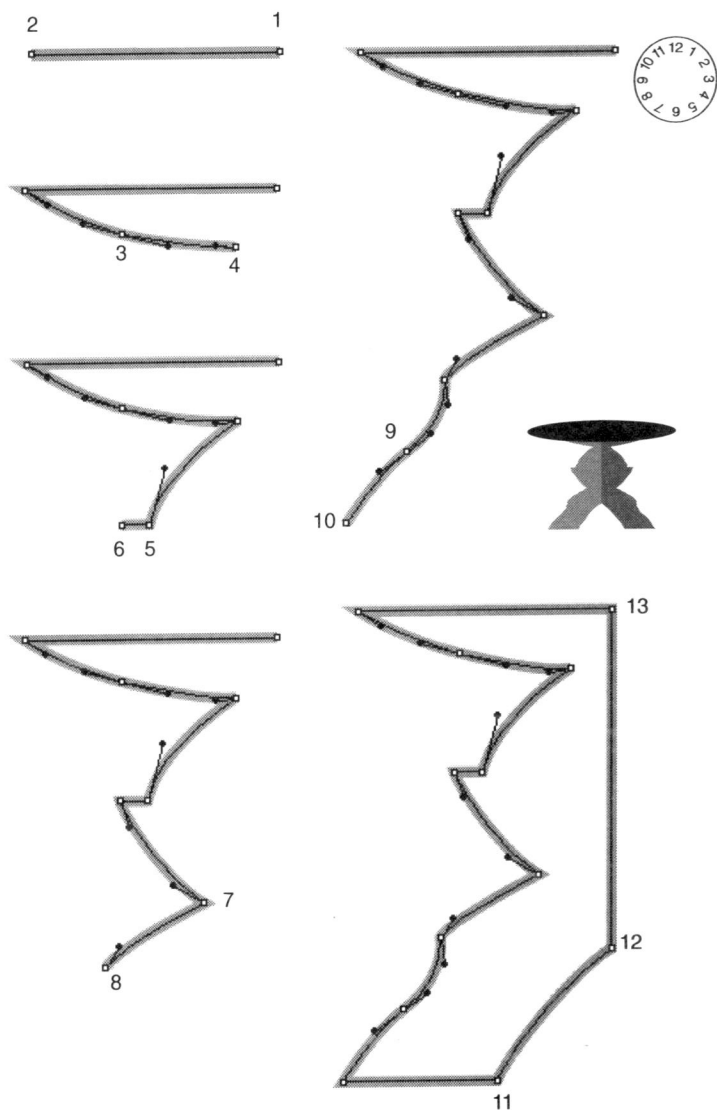

Figure 5.18 Path following the profile of a table support. Viewed in Preview mode with all segments selected for clarity

⑧ Click-drag at 8 o'clock direction to create smooth point. Release mouse. Hold down Alt and click-drag end of leading leading direction line so it's lying in a 5 o'clock direction.

⑨ Click-drag at 7–8 o'clock direction to create smooth point. Release mouse.

⑩ Click-drag at 4 o'clock direction to create smooth point. Release mouse. Hold down Alt and click on point to remove its leading direction line.

⑪ Hold down Shift and click to create corner point level with point. Release mouse and Shift key.

⑫ Click-drag at 2 o'clock direction to create smooth point. Release mouse. Hold down Alt and click on point to remove its leading direction line. Then click on first point (13) to close path.

Editing paths

Pen variants editing tools

There are three pen variants for path editing: Add-anchor-point, Delete-anchor-point and Convert-anchor-point (see Figure 5.19).

Figure 5.19 The Add-anchor-point, Delete-anchor-point and Convert-anchor-point tools

Adding, deleting and converting points

Adding a point

Either:

● With either the Pen or Add-anchor-point tool active, click on path segment. (A small plus sign will appear beside the pen cursor to denote it's over a segment.)

Or:

● Choose Add Anchor Points from the Path sub-menu in the Object menu.

Anchor points will be added midway between existing points.

Deleting a point

● With either the Pen or Remove-anchor-point tool active, click on point. (A small minus sign will appear beside the pen cursor to denote it's over a point.)

▲ With the Remove-anchor-point tool active, hold down the Alt key to switch to the Add-anchor-point tool.

! Press Shift to override the add or remove capabilities of the Pen tool.

Converting a corner point to a smooth point

● With the Convert-direction-point active, click-drag from corner point. The leading direction line will always be the first to emerge.

▲ With the Pen tool active, hold down the Alt key to access this tool.

Converting a smooth point to a corner point

● With the Convert-direction-point active, click on point.

Extending a path

① With the Pen tool active, click on end point. (A small forward slash will appear beside the pen cursor to denote it's over an end point.)

② Click or click-drag to extend path.

▲ The crossed-slash sign on the Pen tool cursor loses its rearward slash, indicating that the Pen tool is positioned over the end point.

Joining two paths

① Select end points to be joined.

② Choose Join from the Path sub-menu in the Object menu.

! If the endpoints are at the same location a single corner point is formed unless two curve points happen to accurately match.

Joining end points of path

● Either:

With the Pen tool active, click on each end point in turn.

Or:

① With one of the selection tools active, select object.

② Choose Join from the Path sub-menu in the Object menu.

Cutting paths

Splitting points

● With the Scissors tool active, click on point.

Splitting segments

● With the Scissors tool active, click on segment.

Splitting objects

● With the Knife tool active, click-drag across filled path, whether open or closed (see Figure 5.20).

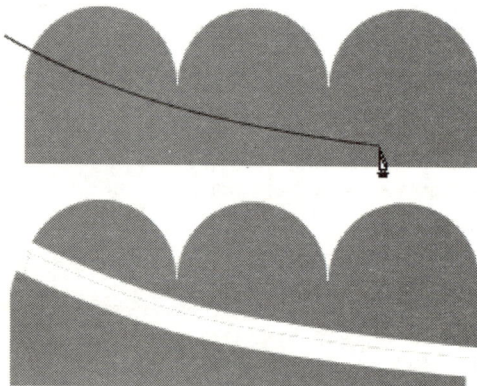

Figure 5.20 Splitting a closed path with the Knife tool (top). Lower part moved away from upper part to illustrate effect (bottom)

Adjusting the line of a path

Moving a point

● With the Direct-direction tool active, click-drag point.

Moving a straight segment

● With the Direct-direction tool active, click-drag segment.

Adjusting a curve segment

With the Direct-direction tool active

Either:

● Click-drag segment.

Or:

● Select segment or associated point and click-drag end of direction handle.

Reshaping paths

You can reshape paths by using the Pencil.

● With one of the selection tools active, click path.

● With the Pencil tool active click-drag from part of a path to another.

You can also reshape – distort – part of path by designating selected anchor points as 'focal' points and click-dragging these points. The focal point(s) move the full distance of the cursor. Non-focal points (any selected points not designated as focal points) move in proportion to the dragged focal point(s) depending on their relative position (see Figure 5.21).

Figure 5.21 Object reshaped by dragging three focal points. Note that the two points immediately to the left of the focal points are moved in proportion to the dragged points

Reshaping a path

① With any selection tool active, select the anchor points on the segment(s) you wish to reshape.

② With the Reshape tool active, click an anchor point you wish to designate as a focal point.

③ Press [Shift] and click on any other points you wish also to designate as focal points.

④ Click-drag any one of the focal points to reshape the path.

Deleting isolated points

Anchor points without associated segments complicate artwork and can slow outputting times. They should therefore be removed on completion of your work.

① Choose Cleanup from the Path sub-menu in the Object menu. The Cleanup dialog box will be displayed.

② Check or tick Stray Points.

③ Click OK.

Applying strokes

Altering the width of a stroke

① Select objects(s).

② Choose Show Stroke from the Window menu. The Stroke palette will be displayed (see Figure 5.22).

③ Enter a value in the Weight field. You can do this by either clicking one of the small triangles or by typing.

④ Click OK to implement a setting you've typed in.

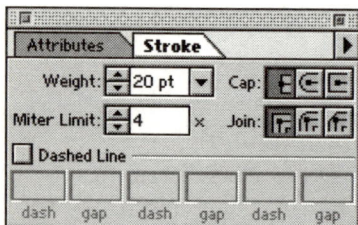

Figure 5.22 Setting a stroke width to 20 pt in the Stroke palette

Dashing a stroke

Creating a dashed stroke involves specifying a value in points for the dash length and gap width (see Figure 5.23). Entering a single value for each aspect, such as 12, 6, will give you a regular dash. Entering more than one value for each aspect, such as 12, 6, 6, 3, 18, 9, will you an irregular dash effect if the three sets of values differ.

① Select objects(s).

② Choose Show Stroke from the Window menu. The Stroke palette will be displayed (see Figure 5.23).

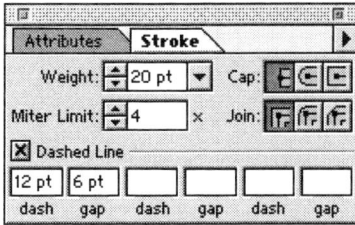

Figure 5.23 Creating a regular dashed line in the Stroke palette.

③ Check or tick Dashed Line.

④ Enter values in the dash and gap fields.

⑤ Press ⏎.

Altering the end treatment of a stroke

① With the Selection tool active, click on object.

② Choose Show Stroke from the Window menu. The Stroke palette will be displayed.

③ Click on one of three Cap types (see Figure 5.24).

Altering the corner treatment of a stroke

① With the Selection tool active, click on object.

② Choose Show Stroke from the Window menu. The Stroke palette will be displayed.

③ Click on one of three Join types (see Figure 5.24).

④ Enter a value in the Miter Limit field (for mitre join only). You can do this by clicking either of the small triangles or by typing. This setting controls when an oblique point becomes bevelled.

Figure 5.24 From left to right: butt cap with miter join, round cap with round join, projecting cap with bevel join

Adding arrowheads

Figure 5.25 Path with and without arrowhead

① With the Selection tool active, click on an open-ended path.

② Choose Add Arrowheads… from the Stylize sub-menu in the Filter menu. The Add Arrowheads dialog box will be displayed (see Figure 5.26).

③ Click on arrows under window to select type of arrowhead.

④ Select options as appropriate (see Figure 5.25).

⑤ Click OK.

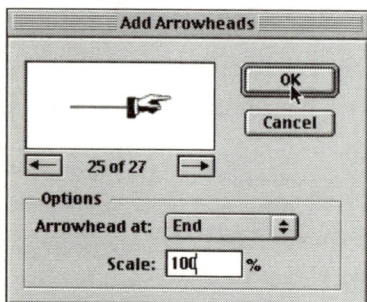

Figure 5.26 Adding an arrowhead

Creating paths from placed images

Occasionally you may wish to trace over an existing drawing or graphic (see Figure 5.27). The Auto trace tool can do this automatically for you provided the image is sufficiently defined. The accuracy of the tool is governed by the Tracing Gap setting in the Type & Auto set of preferences.

Using the Auto trace tool

① Place a bitmap image on the artboard (see Placing images, page 170).

For ease of working, it's best if the image is placed on a layer of its own (see Layering objects, page 89).

② With the Auto trace tool active

Either: click individual shape within image. This way an entire shape within an image is traced.

Or: click-drag from a point at the edge of a shape to another point at the edge. This way only part of a shape is traced.

▲ For greatest accuracy set the tracing gap to zero. A setting of 1 or 2 will ignore gaps in a shape's edges which are 1 or 2 pixels wide.

You can connect a new auto trace path to an existing auto trace path by click-dragging at the anchor point where you wish the paths to join.

Figure 5.27 Tracing part of a rose motif

Summary

Paths All vector objects in Illustrator are composed of segments and points.

Drawing loosely The Pencil and Paintbrush enable freehand drawing of paths and shapes.

Simple shapes Geometric shapes are best achieved by using the range of 'shape' tools in the toolbox.

Drawing accurately Precision drawing is achieved by using the Pen tool.

Curves segments Curves are created by judicious use of direction lines.

Strokes Strokes can be continuous or dashed, their widths can be altered and their end caps and joins styled in one of three ways.

Tracing Simple scanned shapes can be traced automatically using the Auto trace tool.

6 | PAINTING IN COLOUR

Colour can be employed within artworks in many ways: it can give the effect of 3-D form, it can be used in an non-literal way to create pure colour effects, it can support business communications by matching Pantone references, and so on.

Whatever their role, colours in Illustrator, as in other DTP programs, need to be chosen from the correct colour space – mode – for the planned delivery medium.

They need to be accurate on screen so you can make colour decisions with a degree of confidence and they also need to be consistent across the different computer devices used in the workflow.

If you are planning to print your artwork on a conventional press, coloured objects may also need to be prepared to compensate for print misregistration.

So in this chapter I not only cover ways of working with colour in your artworks, I also discuss the various colour modes and libraries available to you.

As importantly, I cover the rudiments of colour management, the need for monitor calibration and trapping basics.

Choosing and applying colours

Colours can be mixed, chosen and applied in a number of ways within Illustrator and can be stored as swatches for repeated use.

When a colour is mixed or chosen, it is shown in one of two overlapping boxes in the toolbox, depending on which of these boxes is active at the time. These two boxes effectively control whether a colour is to be used for painting a fill or for painting a stroke.

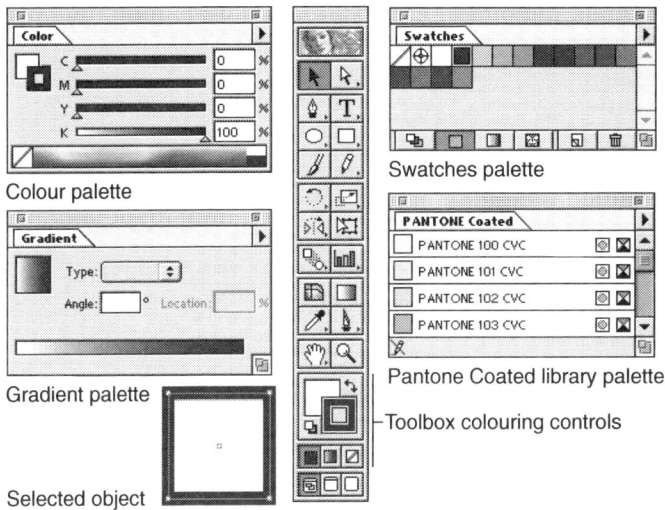

Figure 6.1 Palettes involved in the colouring process

They don't store colours. They are constantly updated when you select colours from palettes, select objects in your illustration or use the Eyedropper tool. If you wish to store colours you drag them into the Swatches palette.

The two boxes in Colour palette update along with those in the toolbox to provide a basis for adjusting colours in one of several colour spaces.

Colours can be applied directly to unselected objects by click-dragging from the toolbox, from the colour palette, from colours in the Swatches and Swatch Library palettes or by using the Paint bucket (see Figure 6.1). If objects are already selected, colours are applied as you mix or choose them.

Painting using the palettes

① Either:

Select any objects if you wish to alter their colours.

The fill and stroke boxes in the toolbox will be updated to match the objects' colours.

Or:

Deselect all objects if you do not wish to alter any of their colours.

The fill and stroke boxes in the toolbox will remain unchanged.

② Select the fill box in the toolbox.

③ Mix a colour in the Colour palette.

Or:

Select on a colour in the Swatches palette.

Or:

Select a colour in one of the Colour Library windows.

④ Select the stroke box in the toolbox.

⑤ Repeat step 3.

!   If selected boxes have different attributes, the fill and/or stroke boxes
    will display a question mark.

▲   Click on the Colour icon in the toolbox to display the Colour palette.

Painting by other means

Applying colours from the toolbox

●   Click-drag from the fill or stroke box in the toolbox over
    any unselected objects (see Figure 6.2).

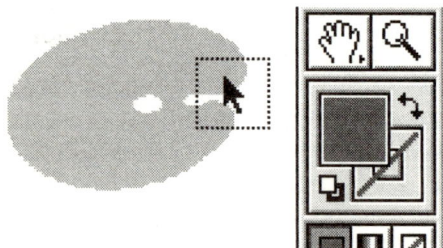

Figure 6.2 Applying a colour from the toolbox

▲   Click on the Switch colours icon (double-ended arrows) at the top right
    of the overlapping boxes in the toolbox to swap the fill and stroke colours
    or press X. The default 'current' colours are black (stroke) and white (fill).

Applying colours using the Paint bucket

The Paint bucket not only paints objects with the current colours in the fill
and stroke boxes, but also applies other object attributes, including stroke

weights. By double-clicking the Paint bucket icon and accessing its tool options, you can limit the range of attributes the tool applies.

● With the Paint bucket tool active, click on any unselected object (see Figure 6.3).

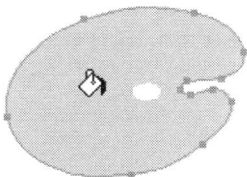

Figure 6.3 Applying a colour using the Paint bucket

Applying no colour

● Click the None icon in the toolbox (see Figure 6.4).

▲ You can also do this by selecting the None swatch in the Swatches palette.

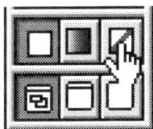

Figure 6.4 Applying transparency within the toolbox

Copying colours from other objects with the Eyedropper

The Eyedropper not only provides a simple way to copy colours, but can also copy other attributes, including stroke weights (see Figure 6.5). By double-clicking its icon and accessing its tool options, you can limit the range of attributes the tool will sample.

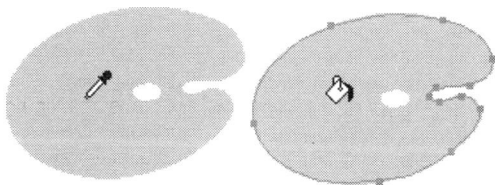

Figure 6.5 Sampling and applying a colour using the Eyedropper

① With the Eyedropper tool active, click on the object whose colour you wish to copy. The fill and stroke boxes in the toolbox will be updated to match the object's colours.

② [Option]-click on the object you wish to re-colour. The Eyedropper icon temporarily turns into the Paint bucket.

Mixing process colours and greys

① Choose Show Colour from the Window menu or click the colour icon in the toolbox (Figure 6.6). The colour palette will be displayed (see Figure 6.7).

Figure 6.6 Clicking the Colour icon to display the Colour palette

② Choose RGB, CMYK or Grayscale in the Colour palette pop-up menu (press the triangle at the top right hand corner of the palette to access this menu).

③ Click once on either the fill box or the stroke box in the toolbox (if the box is already overlapping, there is no need to click it).

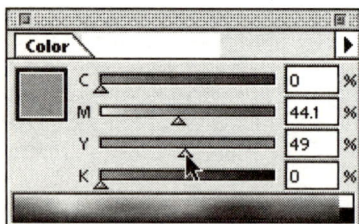

Figure 6.7 Mixing a colour

④ Click a colour within the colour bar on the lower part of palette and/or click-drag the CMYK, RGB or Grayscale sliders above it.

The fill or stroke box in the toolbox will automatically be updated.

If any objects are selected whilst you mix a colour, they will instantaneously be recoloured.

Choosing existing colours

Choosing a colour in the Swatches palette

① Choose Show Swatches from the Window menu. The Swatches palette will be displayed (see Figure 6.8).

② Click once on either the fill box or stroke box in the toolbox (if the box is already overlapping, there is no need to click it).

③ Click a colour within the Swatches palette.

The fill or stroke box in the toolbox will automatically be updated.

If any objects are selected whilst you select a colour, they will instantaneously be recoloured.

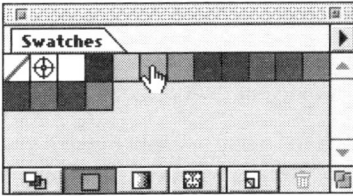

Figure 6.8 Selecting a colour in the Swatches palette

Using library colours

① Choose a library from the Swatch Libraries sub-menu in the Window menu. The library's palette will be displayed (see Figure 6.9).

② Use the scrollbars to view the colour you wish to choose.

③ Select either the fill box or the stroke box in the toolbox (if any objects are selected).

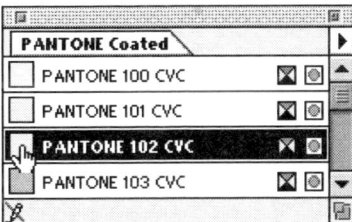

Figure 6.9 Selecting a library colour

④ Click on a colour in the palette. It will automatically be added to the Swatches palette

The fill or stroke box in the toolbox will automatically be updated and any selected objects instantaneously recoloured.

! Selected library colours are automatically added to the Swatches palette.

Creating a palette of colours

Include in the Swatches palette all the colours you plan to use in your art-work. When choosing colours for print always refer to printed colour references, as on-screen colours can be misleading, and specify colours as either process or spot.

It's usually best to clear the Swatches palette of all existing colours, apart from None, white and black, before you add your own colours.

Once all your colours are in place you will be ready to apply them to your artwork. You can, of course, add further colours to the palette as you progress with your work.

Altering the display of swatches

Selecting which swatches are to be dispalyed

● Click on one of the first four display icons at the bottom left of the swatches palette (see Figure 6.10).

Figure 6.10 Display icons at the bottom of the Swatches palette

The first displays all colours, gradients and patterns.

The second displays process and spot colours only.

The third displays gradients only.

The fourth displays patterns only.

Changing the way swatches are presented

● Choose a view from the pop-up menu (see Figure 6.11).

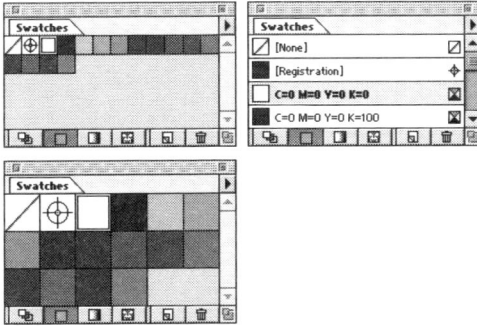

Figure 6.11 The Swatches palette in Small Swatch, Large Swatch and Name view

Removing and adding swatches

Removing existing swatches

① Choose Select all Unused from the Swatches palette pop-up menu (press the triangle at the top right hand corner of the palette to access this menu). Unused swatches will be outlined.

② Click-drag to the Wastebasket in the Swatches palette.

The default black, white and None swatches will automatically be retained.

Use this process to remove any unused colours when you have finished your artwork.

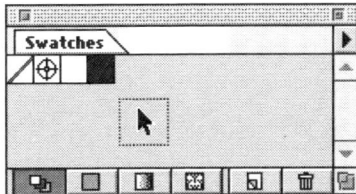

Figure 6.12 Adding a colour by dragging it into the Swatches palette

Adding current fill and stroke colours

① Mix a colour in the Colour palette.

The fill or stroke box in the toolbox will automatically be updated.

② Click-drag the colour from the fill or stroke box into the Swatches palette (see Figure 6.12).

Specifying colours to be process or spot

① Select a colour in the Swatches palette.

② Choose Swatch Options in the Swatches palette pop-up menu (press the triangle at the top right hand corner of the palette to access this menu). The Swatch Options dialog box will be displayed.

③ Choose either Process or Spot in the Colour Mode pop-up menu.

④ Click OK.

▲ A spot within a white triangle on a swatch indicates it's a spot colour.

Removing individual swatches

Use this process to remove the odd unwanted colours as you work.

① Deselect all objects.

② Click-drag swatch to the Wastebasket icon in the Swatches palette (see Figure 6.13).

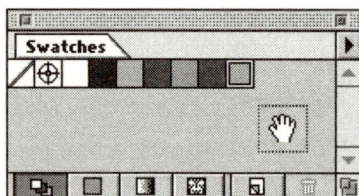

Figure 6.13 Removing a swatch by dragging it into the Trash button

Creating tints of colours

You can create tints of both process and spot colours. This is especially useful if you are working with spot colours and wish to broaden your colour range. By using tints, the number of printing plates is not increased, yet you have more shades at your disposal to use in your artwork.

It's best to make any process colours you intend to tint global. This way not only do they they appear as a single colour in the Colour palette but they also are linked to the base colour to make its easier to control and edit tints (see Adjusting colours throughout an artwork later in this chapter).

Tinting a colour

① Mix or choose a colour by any of the methods described previously..

② Choose Show Colours from the Window menu. The Colour palette will be displayed (see Figure 6.14).

③ Drag the slider to the left. In the case of a non-global process colour, hold down [Shift] and drag the slider that is furthest to the right leftwards. The sliders will move in unison.

The fill or stroke box in the toolbox will automatically be updated.

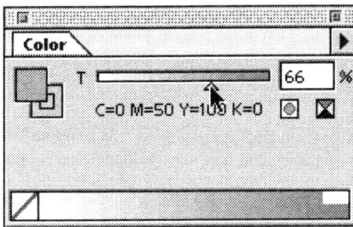

Figure 6.14 Creating a tint of a global colour

④ Save the tinted colour in the Swatches palette. A global tint is saved with the same name as the base colour, but with the tint percentage added to the name.

▲ Click on the Colour icon in the toolbox to display the Colour palette.

! Tints of the same global colour are linked together so if you edit a tint swatch all associated tint swatches and objects painted with those swatches are also changed.

Adjusting colours throughout an artwork

Global colours

Spot colours are, by default, global, i.e. links are automatically created between the colours and any objects to which the colours are assigned. This means that when spot colour swatches are edited, objects containing the colour will automatically be updated wherever they are within your artwork. It's similar to the way style sheets are linked to text within page layout programs. And like style sheets, it enables you to work faster and maintain consistency within complex documents.

Whilst spot colours are automatically global and must remain so, process colours need be specified as global for them to work in this manner.

Specifying process colours to be global

① Select a colour in the Swatches palette.

② Choose Swatch Options in the Swatches palette pop-up menu. The Swatch Options dialog box will be displayed.

③ Choose Process in the Colour Mode pop-up menu if not already selected.

④ Uncheck or untick Non-Global (see Figure 6.15).

⑤ Click OK.

Color Type: | Process Color   ↕ |
            | ☐ Non-Global |

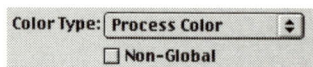

Figure 6.15 Process colour specified as global

▲ A white triangle on a swatch indicates it's a global colour.

Making global changes

You make global changes to colours in an artwork by replacing or altering swatches.

Replacing global swatches

By replacing swatches, you can alter the colour of all objects painted with those swatches.

① Mix a colour in the Colour palette. The fill or stroke box in the toolbox will be updated.

② Hold down [Option] and click-drag the colour from the fill or stroke box over an existing swatch in the Swatches palette.

! To replace a swatch with a library colour, select the colour once it's in the Swatches palette and change it from spot to a process. Then hold down the Alt key and click-drag it over the existing swatch.

Altering global swatches

By altering swatch colours the colours of all objects painted with those swatches are also altered.

① Select a colour in the Swatches palette.

② Choose Swatch Options in the Swatches palette pop-up menu. The Swatch Options dialog box will be displayed (see Figure 6.16).

③ Adjust the colour as required.

④ Click OK.

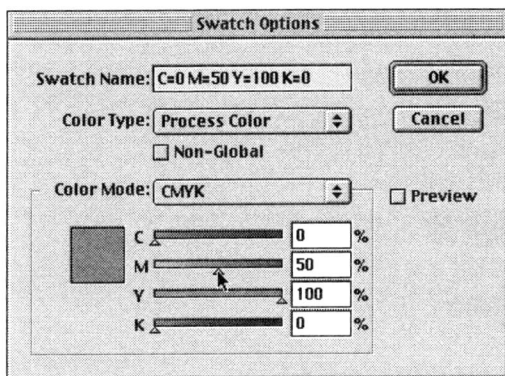

Figure 6.16 Adjusting the colour of a global swatch

Targetting objects with common attributes

Instead of or in addition to altering object colours by making global changes, you can target objects with the same fill and/or stroke.

You may wish to repaint a number of objects sharing the same fill and stroke colours. Instead of repainting each in turn, which takes time and can lead to mistakes, select them all together and alter their colours in one go.

① Select an object with the correct fill and/or stroke.

② Choose Same Paint Style (for same fill and stroke), Same Fill Colour or Same Stroke Colour from the Select sub-menu in the Edit menu.

   Objects with the same attributes will automatically be selected.

③ Apply a new fill and/or stroke colour to the selected objects.

Modifying object colours

Reversing an object's colour

This command creates colour negatives of selected objects and in the process converts their mode to RGB (if not already in so).

① Select object(s).

② Choose Invert Colours from the Colours sub-menu in the Filter menu.

Changing an object's colour values and colour space

Objects painted in RGB, CMYK, grayscale and in tints of global colours can have their colours adjusted and colour spaces switched.

① Select object(s).

② Choose Adjust colours... from the Colours sub-menu in the Filter menu. The Adjust Colours dialog box will be diplayed (see Figure 6.17)

③ Check or tick Preview to preview effect on object(s).

④ Check or tick Convert and select an option in the Colour Mode pop-up menu if you wish to convert objects to one model.

⑤ Uncheck or untick Convert if you wish to adjust the colours in the first colour mode encountered (in case where selected objects are painted with colours from diffent colour modes).

⑥ Check or tick Stroke and Fill as required.

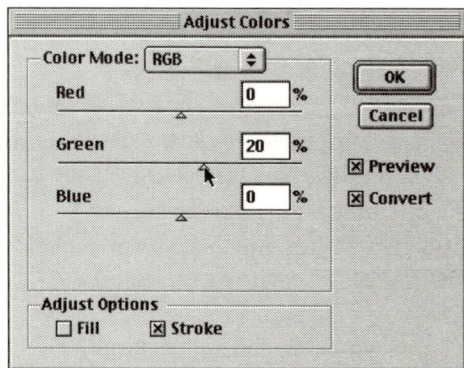

Figure 6.17 Converting and adjusting the stroke colours of several objects

⑦ Click-drag sliders or enter values in fields, as required.

⑧ Click OK.

Changing an object's colour space

Object colours can be switched between process colours at any time.

① Select object(s).

② Choose Convert to RGB, CMYK or Grayscale from the Colours sub-menu in the Filter menu.

Darkening or lightening object colours

① Select object(s).

② Choose Saturate... from the Colours sub-menu in the Filter menu. The Intensity dialog box will be displayed.

③ Check or tick Preview.

④ Moving the slider to the left increases intensity, to the right reduces intensity.

⑤ Click OK.

Filling objects with graduated colour

Applying a saved gradient

① Select any objects to which you wish to apply a gradient.

The fill and stroke boxes in the toolbox will be altered to match the selected objects.

② Choose Show Swatches from the Window menu. The Swatches palette will be displayed (see Figure 6.18).

③ Choose a gradient in the Swatches palette.

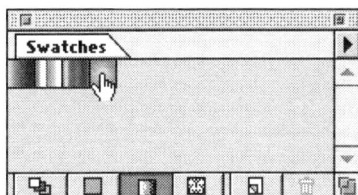

Figure 6.18 Selecting a gradient

! If selected boxes have different attributes, the fill and/or stroke boxes will display a question mark.

Altering the angle of an applied gradient

① Select the Gradient tool.

② Click-drag across the selected item.

Creating a new gradient

Displaying the Gradient palette

Either:

● Choose Show Gradient from the Window menu.

Or:

● Click on the Gradient icon in the toolbox (see Figure 6.19). Either way the Gradient palette will be displayed.

Figure 6.19 Clicking the Gradient icon to display the Gradient palette

Selecting a gradient type

● Choose Radial or Linear from the Type pop-up menu. This attribute can be altered at any time.

Colouring gradient points

① Click on the first small gradient slider beneath the gradient bar. Its triangle will turn black to indicate that it is selected (see Figure 6.20).

② Hold down ⌥[Option] and select a flat colour in the Swatches palette.

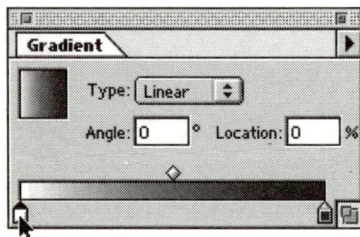

Figure 6.20 Colouring a gradient point

Altering the midpoint position of a gradient

The midpoint dictates the point where gradient colours are 50:50 mix.

● Click-drag the diamond slider above the gradient bar.

Adding further points to a gradient

Multi-coloured gradients can be created for special effects and to model forms with a greater degree of realism. You can, for instance, create a gradient with areas of highlight, shadow and reflected light to give a cylindrical object a 3-D look.

● Click below the gradient bar (see Figure 6.21).

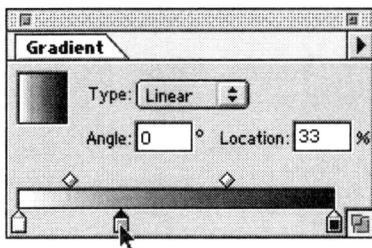

Figure 6.21 Adding a new colour point

Saving a new gradient

● Click-drag the gradient from the Gradient palette or the fill or stroke box (in the toolbox) into the Swatches palette. Hold down [Option] if you wish to replace an existing swatch with a new colour.

Working with colour modes

The colours you use within Illustrator should be selected from the correct colour space – mode – before they are applied to objects.

The space will be determined by the delivery medium and colour availability, i.e. whether artwork is to be viewed on screen or printed and how many and which colours are to be used.

For Web or multimedia images, colours should be in RGB, and either mixed within the colour palette (in RGB setting) or selected from one of the RGB libraries. The RGB colours are used by computer monitors to display full-colour work on-screen. They offer a very wide colour gamut, allowing you to choose colours of a high saturation.

For printed artwork, colours can either be mixed in the colour palette (in CMYK setting) or selected from one of the proprietary colour libraries. However you select them, they can be specified as either process or spot.

The CMYK colours are the colours used by many desktop printers and digital/web offset presses to reproduce full-colour photographs and illustrations. Colours mixed from these colours should therefore reproduce accurately in print.

RGB libraries

Use the System (Windows or Macintosh) and/or Web palettes for indexed artwork intended for multimedia and Web documents – in fact for any documents intended solely for on-screen display.

The System palettes comprise 256 colours whilst the Web palette comprises 216 so-called Web-safe colours. All three libraries are essentially sub-sets of the RGB colour space (represented in its entirety within the Illustrator's Colour palette).

Proprietary print libraries

The Pantone Coated and Uncoated Libraries were originally designed for artwork intended for print. Nowadays, they are widely used as a method of colour selection whatever the target medium and for both spot or process reproduction.

The two ranges are essentially the same, except the latter are slightly darker than the former to simulate the deepening of colours on uncoated stock. Only a small percentage of the colours can be simulated using process inks. Because of this, colour shifts usually occur when converting to CMYK.

Pantone Process, on the other hand, solely uses colours with CMYK equivalents. You can therefore confidently use them as a basis for selecting CMYK mixes.

The Trumatch library contains over 2000 achievable computer-generated colours. Like Pantone Process it's a sub-set of the CMYK colour space so use it as another way of selecting CMYK colours for print.

Process or spot

Both CMYK mixes and proprietary colours can be specified as either process or spot. Process colours involve four printing plates for outputting on a printing press whilst each spot colour requires its own dedicated plate – it's printed as a separate ink.

▲ Specify spot for any additional colour to black for printed matter using only two or three colours, or as an additional colour to the process colours, when a process equivalent is not accurate enough.

Specify process for all colours for printed matter incorporating full colour pictures, unless a process equivalent is not accurate enough. Every spot colour in addition to the process colours will substantially increase printing costs.

Process colours are printed using the CMYK colours, whichever colour space is used to specify the colour.

❗ Avoid altering a given Pantone name if spot colour is specified and you are planning to import your artwork into a page layout program.

The colour white

White represents the white of the screen or the colour of the paper you are printing on, whether it's pure white or not. Objects painted white will have opaque white backgrounds, so when they are placed over other objects, the white of the screen or 'white' paper will show.

If you wish to print white for silkscreen purposes, create a pale colour (any colour will do) and specify it as a spot colour. You can then inform your printer that this colour represents white and they will then use a white ink when screening the colour.

Transparent fills

If objects are given a None fill and placed over other items, the underlying items will show through. Transparency is also achieved by compounding (see page 114).

Ensuring accurate colour

One of the methods Illustrator uses to ensure accurate colour across different output devices – monitor screens, digital printers, printing presses and so on – is based on the use of ICC profiles, an industry-wide colour space description defined by the International Colour Consortium (ICC).

Illustrator uses a colour management module (CMM) to interpret the profiles that describe RGB and CMYK colour spaces. You can choose between three colour management systems (CMS) to convert images, although Adobe recommends its own Adobe CMS.

External images are not managed by such systems, so if you wish bitmap images within artworks to be faithfully reproduced, embed rather than link when you place or paste them within an Illustrator document.

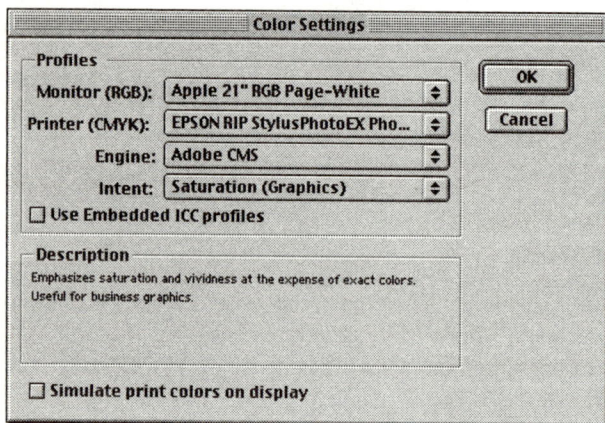

Figure 6.22 The Colour Settings dialog box

Changing the colour settings

① Choose Colour Settings from the File menu. The Colour Settings dialog box will be displayed (see Figure 6.22).

② Choose the monitor and printer you are using from the Monitor and Printer pop-up menus.

③ Choose Adobe CMS from the Engine pop-up menu.

④ Choose either Perceptual (for continuous tone images) or Saturation (for flat graphics) from the Intent pop-up menu.

⑤ Check or tick Use Embedded ICC profiles if you wish the file to be saved with its profile. This is only necessary if you plan to work on a document on another computer.

⑥ Check or tick Simulate print colours on display if you wish your monitor to simulate colours as they will appear printed.

⑦ Click OK.

! ICC profiles can be embedded only if documents are saved in PDF, TIFF, JPEG or Photoshop 5 format.

Calibrating your monitor

Whilst the monitor setting in the Colour Settings dialog box informs Illustrator about the type of monitor you are using, it does not in itself influence the way your monitor displays colour.

Accuracy of colour on screen is controlled by the Adobe Gamma utility which lets you calibrate contrast, brightness, gamma (midtones), colour balance and white point.

The calibration need be done only once and will be appropriate for the other programs you use.

The Adobe Gamma utility is located in the Adobe folder within the Common files folder within the Program files in Windows and in the Control panels folder on the Macintosh. The utility is assisted and takes you on a step-by-step basis throughout the calibration process.

Colour misregistration and how it is avoided

Hairline gaps can sometimes appear between coloured items when documents are printed on conventional presses. This problem, faced by all those working in print, is due to printing plate misregistration and paper stretch during printing.

Although such gaps are particularly apparent when spot colours are used, it's less of a problem with process colours for two reasons: firstly the halftone screens employed to provide the percentage tints slightly soften the edges of coloured objects and thus partially mask any gaps; secondly any process colours common to overlapping objects provide a continuous 'bridge' between objects. Both these factors help to minimize the impact of misregistration if it occurs.

To allow for misregistration object colours need to slightly overlap. The amount of overlap – trap – needs to be agreed with your printer, who alone knows the optimum amounts for his presses. As a general guide, offset litho work normally requires a trap of 0.0125 pt and silkscreen work a trap of 0.1–0.2 mm

There's no need to worry about trapping when outputting to digital colour printers/presses or when exporting images for Web pages as no printing plates are involved and therefore misregistration is not an issue. However, the trapping of coloured artworks imported into other page layout programs does need to be addressed.

Trapping approaches

There are four approaches to trapping in Illustrator:

- Not trapping at all.
- Trapping with intermediate objects using the Pathfinder Trap filter.
- Trapping with spread/choked strokes.
- Leaving the trapping to others.

Not trapping at all

There is no need to trap if colour areas don't butt or overlap. This applies to both process and spot colours.

There is also no need to trap if butted and overlapped process colour share common colour components even if they are of different percentage strengths (see Figure 6.23).

You can also sometimes get away without trapping on an offset litho press if the run is short, the colours are all process and the machine minder is diligent. This depends very much on the dedication and professionalism of the printing company you use.

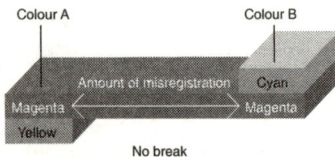

Figure 6.23 Common magenta component within object colours A, B and C obviates the need for trapping. Colours shown in section view

Trapping using the Pathfinder Trap filter

This is perhaps the easiest trapping method to implement as Illustrator processes the traps for you. It does so by creating additional trapping objects where colours abut (see Figure 6.24).

It's a perfect method for trapping less complex artworks where object numbers are fairly low. But it has a downside as artworks can be difficult to alter once such traps are in place.

Having said this, the trap filter should be a beginner's first point of call.

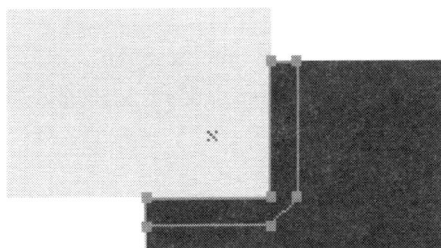

Figure 6.24 Trap object overlaying darker of two rectangles

① Select two or more overlapping objects in your artwork.

② Choose Pathfinder from the Window menu. The Pathfinder palette will be displayed.

③ Click the Trap icon (Figure 6.25). The Pathfinder Trap dialog box will be displayed (see Figure 6.26).

Figure 6.25 Selecting the Pathfinder Trap

④ Enter the total trap amount (in points) in the Thickness field.

⑤ Enter a value in the Height/Width field to specify a trap on horizontal lines as a percentage of the trap on vertical lines. A value other than 100 takes into account uneven paper stretch.

⑥ Enter 40 in Tint reduction to reduce the values of lighter colours being trapped.

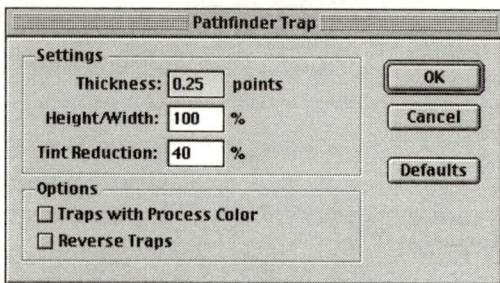

Pathfinder Trap
Settings
Thickness: [0.25] points
Height/Width: [100] %
Tint Reduction: [40] %
Options
☐ Traps with Process Color
☐ Reverse Traps

Figure 6.26 The Pathfinder Trap dialog box

⑦ Uncheck or untick Traps with Process Color if you wish to convert spot colour traps to equivalent process colours.

⑧ Uncheck or untick Reverse Traps to trap darker colours into lighter colours. This option does not work with blacks containing one or more other colours.

⑨ Click OK.

! Any dramatic increase in object numbers resulting from such trapping may affect outputting times and can prevent a document from outputting.

Trapping with spread/choked strokes

Trapping by spreading and choking strokes is a more streamlined method than trapping using the Pathfinder filter as it's more economical in terms of object use. It is also better for trapping type which has been converted to outlines.

However, it does sometimes require some ingenuity to successfully trap objects by this means. Since this is a beginners' book, I will cover only the basics of this method.

Figure 6.27 A spread trap (left) and a choked trap (right). The tones of strokes have been altered to distinguish them from object fills

Spreading and choking is achieved through the overprinting of coloured strokes around objects (see Figure 6.27). In all cases it is the foreground object that is manipulated for this purpose.

Trapping shapes

① Select the foreground object.

② Apply a stroke to the object and set its width to twice the intended trap amount.

③ Either:

Spread the stroke by painting it the same colour as its fill.

Or:

Choke the stroke by painting it the same colour as the background object's fill.

④ Check or tick Overprint Stroke in the Attributes palette (see Figure 6.28).

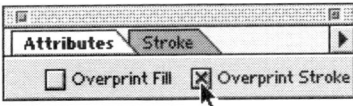

Figure 6.28 Setting a stroke to overprint in the Attributes palette

The difference between spreading and choking

When you spread, the foreground object increases in size to overlap the edges of the hole knocked out of the background object (see Figure 6.29). Depending on the amount of trap, its size increase may or may not be apparent to the eye.

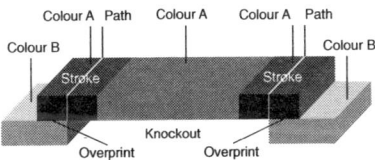

Figure 6.29 A spread trap. Upper object stroke colour A traps (overprints) lower object colour B by half the width of its stroke

When you choke, the hole that is knocked out of the background object is slightly decreased in size to underlap the edges of the foreground object (see Figure 6.30). Any size decrease will not be obvious as it's hidden by the foreground object.

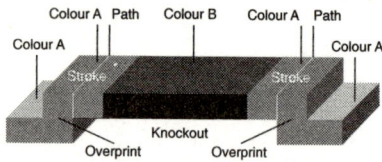

Figure 6.30 A choked trap. Upper object stroke colour A traps (overprints) lower object colour B by half the width of its stroke

As objects usually overlay more than one object within an artwork, spreading is the more useful of the two options despite the inevitable increase in object size. This is less discernible if foreground object colours are fairly light. If not, choking may be the only option open to you. It's more complicated to set up when different background colours are present as it involves the use of masked duplicates (see Figure 6.31). To demonstrate the use of masks for this purpose, I show you how to trap an object against another object and the artboard.

Trapping across colours

① Create a background object on Layer 1 with a fill colour but no stroke (represented by a rectangle in Figure 6.31).

② Create a foreground object on Layer 2 also with a fill colour but no stroke (represented by a circle).

③ Duplicate both layers and stack the four layers in this order:

Layer 1 copy (rectangle)

Layer 2 copy (circle)

Layer 2 (circle)

Layer 1 (rectangle).

④ Hide Layers 1 and 2 and select the rectangle and circle on the two visible layers (Layer 1 copy and Layer 2 copy).

⑤ Choose Make from the Masks sub-menu in the Object menu. The rectangle now masks the circle.

⑥ With the Selection tool active, select the circle and set its width to twice the proposed trapping amount. Set its stroke to match the fill colour of the rectangle on Layer 1.

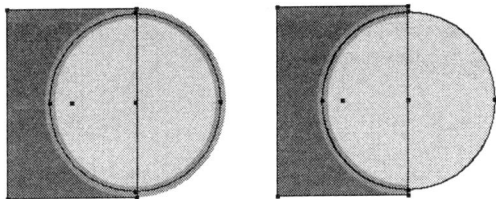

Figure 6.31 Unmasked effect (left) and masked effect (right). The masked circle is represented by two circles. The left side of one is seen within the coloured rectangle. The right hand side of the other is seen to its right. As one is directly on top of the other they appear to be the same circle. The tones of strokes have been altered to distinguish them from object fills

    ⑦ Deselect the circle and show all layers.

    Now the stroke of the circular foreground object traps against the rectangular background object without its stroke appearing elsewhere.

Trapping lines

Trapping lines – paths without fills – is less straightforward than trapping shapes as it always involves the creation of duplicate paths. This is necessary as you cannot apply two different path attributes to a single line.

As with filled paths, you can spread or choke lines. To minimize the visual impact of the increases in line width where possible adhere to the following rule: spread strokes where light foreground colours are against dark backgrounds and choke strokes where dark foreground colours are against light backgrounds.

Spreading strokes

To spread strokes a thickened duplicate path is coloured to match the original line and set to overprint. The original line is not specified to overprint.

    ① Duplicate the layer containing the path.

    ② Position the duplicated layer above the original layer.

    ③ Select the path on the duplicate layer and increase the width of its stroke by twice the proposed trapping amount.

    ④ Check or tick Overprint Stroke in the Attributes palette.

The original line now knocks a hole in the background object and the duplicate of the line spreads to slightly beyond the edges of the knockout.

Choking strokes

To choke strokes a thinned duplicate path is coloured to match the original line and sent behind the original. The original line is set to overprint.

① Select the stroked path.

② Check or tick Overprint Stroke in the Attributes palette.

③ Duplicate the layer containing the path.

④ Position the duplicated layer below the original layer.

⑤ Select the path on the duplicate layer and decrease the width of its stroke by twice the proposed trapping amount.

The duplicate line, being narrower than the original line, knocks out an area that is slightly narrower than the original line, creating a choke.

Trapping using a dedicated trapping program

If you find trapping far too complicated, you can always leave it to your repro house to handle. They will either trap using one of the two methods I've discussed or they will apply trapping at a bitmap level when outputting films.

Summary

Colours Choose colours from a colour space suitable for the planned delivery medium.

Toolbox The toolbox provides a control for targeting fills and strokes, for switching between flat colours and gradients.

Eyedropper and Paint bucket These tools work in unison to sample and paint objects as well as to apply other visual attributes.

Mixing colours Colours can be mixed in the Colour palette in one of several colour spaces.

Saving colours Any colours you mix or select can be saved in the Swatches palette for repeated use.

Colour fidelity Accurate on-screen colour is achieved by establishing the correct colour setup and by fine-tuning monitor settings.

Trapping Trapping may be necessary for artworks intended for print.

7 | SELECTING AND LAYERING OBJECTS

Before you can work on any object in Illustrator, you have to select it. Whilst this is possibly one of the more frequent Illustrator actions, it can also be one of the trickiest. Anchor points and paths, being finely detailed, are easy to miss with the cursor, and when many objects are positioned within close proximity to one another it's often very difficult to select the object you want even in Preview Artwork mode. This is especially the case when paths and anchor points share the same location.

Part of the answer lies in the organization of objects into layers (I cover the crucial role they play in efficient artwork production later in this chapter).

The rest lies in knowing the correct procedures for selecting objects, whatever their situation on the artboard.

Selecting objects

Selection tools are used to select points, segments, paths, sub-groups and groups for subsequent treatment.

There are three of these tools and several menu commands within Illustrator. Each selects objects in different ways. Used in combination, any object can be selected, given time and patience.

Selection tools

There are three selection tools: Selection, Direct-selection and Group-selection (Figure 7.1). Each selects in a different way.

Figure 7.1 The Selection, Direct-selection and Group-selection tools

Selection tool

This tool selects objects and groups of objects.

▲ Memory aid: solid icon denotes complete object(s).

Direct-selection tool

This tool selects points and segments – effectively parts of a path. It also selects objects if their centre points are clicked, provided Area Select is checked or ticked in the General set of preferences.

▲ Memory aid: outline of icon denotes paths.

Group-selection tool

This tool selects grouped objects and linked type containers (see Grouping items together, page 102).

▲ Memory aid: + sign signifies objects joined or linked together.

Selection techniques

Selecting grouped objects

Selecting groups

● With the Selection tool active, click within group.

Selecting sub-groups

You can select groups within groups for subsequent treatment or copying. This technique is particularly useful when painting parts of graphs.

● With the Group-selection tool active, click on sub-group.

Each additional click selects the next enclosing group. Anchor points on objects within selected sub-groups will show as solid squares (see Figure 7.2).

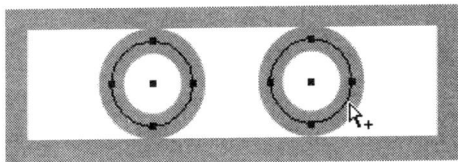

Figure 7.2 Selecting sub-groups with groups

Selecting objects

● With the Selection tool active, click object. The anchor points on a selected object will show as solid squares.

Selecting segments

You can select parts of a path for subsequent manipulation or copying by either selecting segments directly or by selecting their intervening anchor points. The former way allows you to select a single segment only. The latter way always involves the selection of pairs of segments. Since segments must have end points these automatically become part of any selection.

Selecting a single segment

● With the Direct-selection tool active, click on segment (see Figure 7.3). Adjacent anchor points remain as open squares.

Figure 7.3 Selecting segment by clicking on path

Selecting segment pairs

This technique selects segments either side of a point together with their associated end points. The segments remain connected.

● With Direct-selection tool active, click on intervening point (see Figure 7.4). The anchor point will show as a solid

square. The segments either side of a point will be selected,
along with their associated end points.

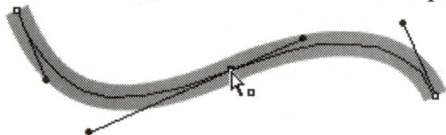

Figure 7.4 Selecting segments by clicking on point

Selecting points

Selecting a point

● With Direct-selection tool active, click on a nearby segment
and then click on point. A selected anchor point will show as
a solid square.

Selecting all or no objects

Selecting an entire artwork

Either:

● Choose Select All from the Edit menu

Or:

● Press ⌘+A.

Deselecting an entire artwork

Either:

● Click somewhere on the image with any selection tool.

Or:

● Choose Select None from the Edit menu or press ⌘
Shift+A.

Selecting non-selected objects

● Choose Inverse from the Select sub-menu in the Edit menu.

Selecting by marqueeing

Selecting multiple objects

● With the Selection tool active, click-drag from a point on
the blank area of the artboard diagonally across all the items
to be selected.

Selecting parts of multiple objects

● With the Direct-selection tool active, click-drag from a point on the blank area of the artboard diagonally across all the parts to be selected.

Extending and reducing selections

Adding to a selection

● Hold down [Shift] and click on item you wish to add to the current selection(s).

Subtracting from a selection

● Hold down [Shift] and click on item you wish to subtract from the current selection(s).

Selecting on basis of colour and weight

You can select objects which have the same fill and stroke colours, fill colour, stroke colour and stroke weight.

① Select an object with the target attributes.

② Choose an option from the Select sub-menu in the Edit menu.

Objects with the same attributes will automatically be selected.

Layering objects

All artwork, other than the most basic, should be created using layers. These are analogous to the sheets of clear acetate artists use to animate cartoons (see Figure 7.5).

Using layers offers the following benefits:

● Object selection is made much easier as you can isolate objects on a layer-by-layer basis.

● You are less likely to accidentally alter parts of an artwork as layer objects can be locked.

● Visualization is made easier as you can show only those layers you wish to view or preview.

- Moving objects in front of and behind each other is facilitated as you can change the order of layers. You don't need to rely on the stacking order of objects within layers.

- Using the clipboard is easier as you can select target layers for pasting into.

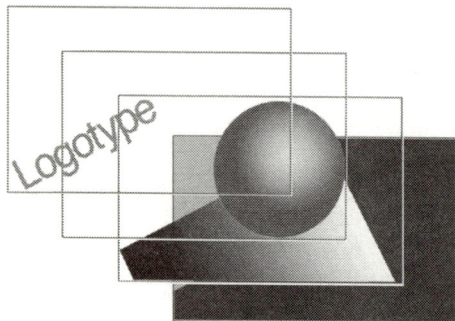

Figure 7.5 Artwork showing build-up of four layers

In fact there is no good argument for not using layers. They don't in themselves create any extra work and, unlike its sister program Photoshop, you leave the layers intact when your work is completed.

Working with multiple layers

When you start a document, only a single layer (called Layer 1) is provided for you to work on. You need to create additional layers before you start beginning an artwork for the reasons I've just listed (see Figure 7.6).

If you analyse most work, it consists of background objects such as coloured panels, midground objects comprising the main subject matter, and foreground objects such as type. These objects can (and should) be given their own layers.

For instance, before you add type, create a layer and name it 'type'. Then with the layer selected add your type matter.

You can create additional layers as you work, duplicate layers, delete layers you don't need, change the order of layers and move objects between layers.

Colour illustrations

The seven illustrations in this colour section are intended to provide a context for some of the techniques and processes covered elsewhere in this book. I used layers to organize artwork objects in all cases and the Pathfinder commands quite a lot to create complicated shapes from more simple drawn objects. I've used compounding in one illustration to create a hole effect and blending in another to model an object. Superimposed paths have come in handy to create parallel lines in one illustration. For both the patterned object and graph artworks I created my own designs to create my own custom swatches and column designs.

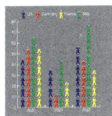

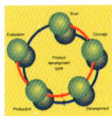

Hole in block

This illustration of a wedge-shaped block and ball has been drawn using the Pen tool and Ellipse tools.
The petal-shaped hole was created by overlapping two circles (A) and applying the Intersect Pathfinder to remove the areas which are not overlapping. The resultant object was compounded with the object representing the front of the block to create the effect of a hole. The shape below the hole was created by applying the Minus Front Pathfinder to copies of the original overlapping circles. A linear gradient fill was applied to this shape (B). The ball was created using the Ellipse tool and modelled by giving the circular object a radial gradient fill.

Order of layers:
Ball
Wedge
Background

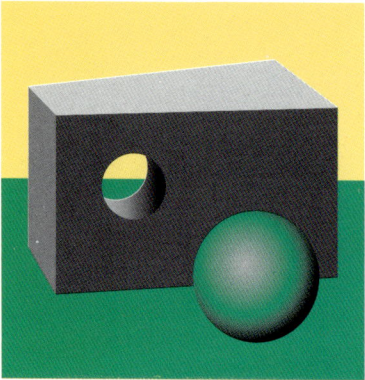

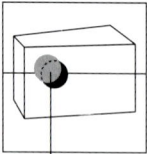

A   B   C

Task lamp

The metal lampshade started off as two rotated ellipses. The side of the shade was drawn using the Pen tool (A). All three items were then copied. The side of the shade was edited using the Minus Front and Minus Back Pathfinders in conjunction with the two ellipses. This edited shape would later be used as a mask (C). Three blend shapes were created using the Pen tool (B). These shapes were then selected and blended to give modelling to the shade. The outline shape created earlier was placed over the blend and selected with it. A mask was made to hide unwanted areas of the blend. The lightbulb was created using the Ellipse tool and then given a radial gradient fill.

Name and stacking of layers:
Lamp Mask
Lamp Blend
Desk
Room

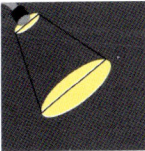

A

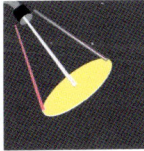

B

C

Logotype

This logo started off as two lines of type set with negative tracking and leading (A). The type was converted to outlines and released from a compounded state (B). A background square was created using the Rectangle tool (C). All the objects were then selected and trimmed using the Trim Pathfinder. This process converted all the areas which were overlapping to separate objects. These were then individually coloured.

Order of layers:
Type
Square

A   B   C

Patterned cube

The logo in this design was built up from a number of shapes snapped to a grid created by the Rectangle and Ellipse tools. The corners of the large central rectangle were radiused using the Round Corners filter (A). The shapes were then reduced in number by using the Merge Pathfinder and then coloured (B). The resultant artwork was copied and reduced in size using the Scale tool. It was then defined as a pattern design within the Edit menu. The front face of the cube was created using the Rectangle tool. It was then assigned the pattern fill. It was then copied twice. Each copy was scaled, horizontally for the right face and vertically for the top face (C). Both were sheared to a 45° angle (D).

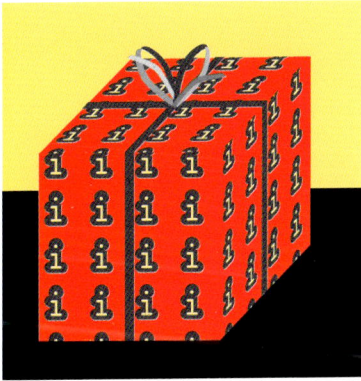

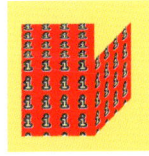

A   B   C   D

Manpower graph

This chart started off as standard 40 mm square column graph with data as shown (A). The man device was drawn separately as two closed paths using the Pen and Ellipse tools (B). Four copies were made of this device (C), with each copy given a different fill colour and no stroke. Each copy was, in turn, defined as a design within the Graph Design dialog box. By selecting sub-groups within the graph (grouping legend rectangle and related columns), each design was incorporated as a column within the Column dialog box. A repeating column type was specified, with rotated legend. Each design was specified to represent 10 units, with fractions being represented as chopped designs.

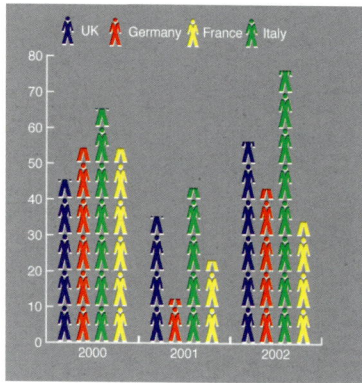

A		UK	Germany	Italy	France
	"2000"	45	54	65	54
	"2001"	35	12	43	23
	"2002"	56	43	76	34

B

C

Process diagram

The spiral effect began as a circle reflected about its horizontal axis. Its upper anchor point was split using the Scissors tool. Using the Reshape tool the split anchor point was dragged upwards and to the left to create the spiral's blue segments (the circle's three other anchor points were selected whilst the tool was applied) (A). A copy of the reshaped path was then positioned to create the spiral's red segments (B). A ball was then created by blending two circles (B). It was positioned along with nine copies along the spiral's path (C). Type was then added to label the balls. Layers were used to assist in the stacking of the objects so that the correct spatial arrangement was achieved.

Order of layers:
Globes 2
Spiral 2
Globes1
Spiral 1
Background

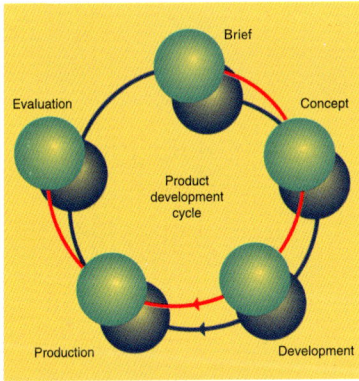

A

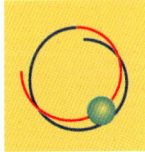

B

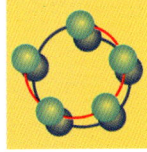

C

Dog with lines

The dog was drawn on the Dog Fill layer using the Pencil tool. Its closed path was given a white fill only (A). Several closed paths were then loosely drawn on the Patches layer (B). The Dog layer was duplicated. This new layer was named Crop. All the layers were locked except the Crop and Patches layers. All visible items were then selected and cropped using the Crop Pathfinder. After unlocking the other layers the Dog layer was duplicated again. This new layer, named Dog Stroke, was moved above the other layers and its path given a black stroke. Jagged lines were drawn on the Jagged Outline layer using the Pen tool. Stroke was set to 5 pt, coloured black and given a projecting cap. This layer was duplicated to create another layer. This new layer, was named Jagged Inline. The stroke of the duplicated lines was narrowed to 3 pt and coloured white (C).

Order of layers:
Dog Stroke
Crop
Patches
Jagged Inline
Jagged Outline
Dog Fill
Square

A

B

C

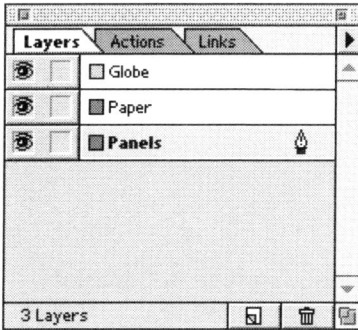

Figure 7.6 Layers palette listing three named layers

Working with layers

Showing the Layer palette

● Choose Show Layers from the Window menu.

Adding a new layer

● Click the New Layer icon at the bottom of the Layers palette (see Figure 7.7).

Or:

● Hold down ⌥Option and click the New Layer icon at the bottom of the Layers palette. This way you can pre-select options for the new layer.

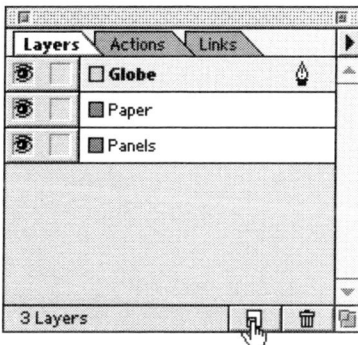

Figure 7.7 Adding a new layer

▲ To retrospectively alter a layer's options, select the layer and choose Options for Layer '...' in the palette's pop-up menu or double-click layer name. Re-specify options as required.

Duplicating a layer

● Click-drag its layer name to New layer icon at the bottom of the palette.

Deleting a layer

● Click its layer name and either click-drag to Wastebasket icon or click Wastebasket icon (see Figure 7.8).

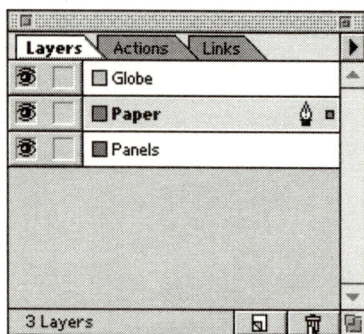

Figure 7.8 Deleting a layer

Changing the order of layers

● Click-drag the layer name or thumbnail up or down within the Layers palette (see Figure 7.9).

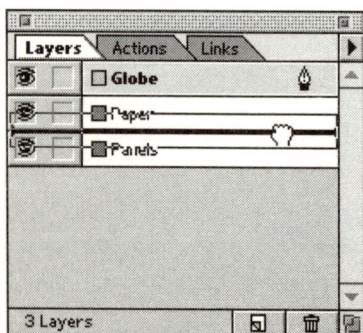

Figure 7.9 Changing the order of layers

Moving objects between layers

① Select the object(s) to be moved.

② Click-drag the small square to the right of the current layer name up or down the list to align with the destination layer (see Figure 7.10).

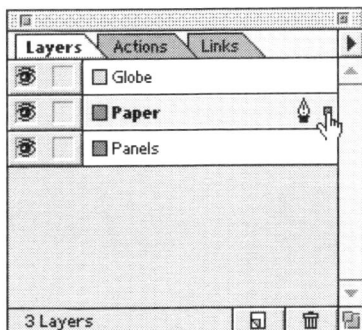

Figure 7.10 Moving selected objects between layers

Altering the attributes of layers

Hiding and showing a layer

● Click the 'eye' icon to the far left of the layer name to remove icon. All items on the layer will now be hidden.

● Click same area to redisplay icon. All items on the layer will be reshown.

Locking all layer objects

This command protects objects from being inadvertently edited. By locking a layer you can confidently work on other layers without having to worry about disturbing work elsewhere.

● Click the layer name and click to right of the 'eye' icon. The presence of 'pencil with strike through' icon indicates that a layer is locked.

Altering the view mode of a layer

This technique toggles between Preview and Artwork view modes.

● Click the layer name, press down [⌘] and click the 'eye' icon.

Preventing a layer from printing

● Double-click the layer name and uncheck or untick Print. Click OK.

Renaming a layer

① Double-click the layer name. The Layer Options dialog box will be displayed (see Figure 7.11).

② Enter a new name in the Name field.

③ Click OK.

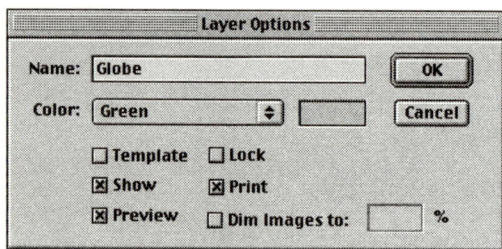

Figure 7.11 The Layers Options dialog box

Manipulating objects on different layers

All manipulations will work across layers, except those involving the joining points and paths.

Points and paths on different levels, when joined, are automatically moved to the uppermost layer.

Altering the stacking within layers

All objects, including grouped objects, have a stacking order. Older objects always underlap newer ones when you position them together on a layer. This is the way PostScript works. You can alter the stacking order at any time for either access or composing purposes.

Changing the stacking order of items

① With the Selection tool active, click the item to be moved.

② Choose an option from the Arrange sub-menu in the Object menu.

Pasting in front of/behind selected objects

When you paste objects, you can paste them directly in front of or directly behind a selected object.

① First cut or copy the object to be pasted as described in Chapter 8).

② Select the object you wish to paste in front of or behind.

③ Choose Paste in Front or Paste in Back from the Edit menu.

▲ Multiple selections moved this way retain their stacking order in relation to each other.

Summary

Selection tools The Selection, Direct-selection and Group-selection tools enable you to select whole objects, part-objects and object sub-groups.

Selection commands Objects can be selected on the basis of their fill and stroke colours and also on the basis of their stroke weights.

Benefits of layers Layers ease object selection and movement and aid visualization.

Use of layers Create a new layer for each type of artwork content and for discrete object groupings.

Selection colours Set the selection colours for each layer to stand out against your artwork colours.

Paths When paths on different layers are joined, they move to the uppermost of the two layers.

Objects Selected objects on a layer are moved to another layer by vertically dragging the small square in the Layers palette.

Artwork completion There is no need to remove layers on completion of an artwork.

8 | TRANSFORMING OBJECTS

Illustrator caters for just about every transformation and copying requirement you can think of. You can move, scale, rotate, reflect and shear (skew) objects or copies of objects, from their centre points or from points you designate yourself, and with pinpoint accuracy.

The use of transformations saves time and helps to reduce inconsistencies in your artwork. Rather than having to draw similar objects from scratch all you need to do is to transform copies of objects instead.

You not only work faster this way but you also ensure that objects are scaled or sheared correctly. And since copied parts share attributes with their originals, consistency is maintained.

For instance, if you need to create a side face for a cube, create a copy of its front face and shear the copy. If you need to create a symmetrical object, create one side first, copy it and then reflect the copy to create the opposite side.

Transformed copies can be accurately positioned and/or joined with other objects to complete the desired effect.

Moving objects

Objects can be repositioned using:

- the mouse
- the cursor keys
- the Move command
- the Transform palette
- the Align palette

Moving objects with the mouse

The simplest way to reposition objects is to drag them with the mouse; this need not be inaccurate as objects can be snapped to guides, grids or objects.

Dragging objects

● With the appropriate selection tool active, select objects(s). Click-drag to new location.

Snapping objects to ruler guides

You can snap objects to ruler guides with Snap to Point enabled.

● With the Selection tool active, select objects(s). Click-drag to guide.

The cursor automatically becomes outlined when positioned over a guide to denote that part of the object being dragged will snap to a guide.

Snapping points to points

You can snap anchor points to other anchor points with Snap to Point enabled.

● With the Direct-selection tool active, select an anchor point. Click-drag over the anchor point on another path (not end point).

The cursor automatically becomes outlined when positioned over a guide to denote that part of the object being dragged will snap to a guide.

▲ If you wish to drag an object, such as a point, close to a guide without snapping to it, you can temporarily disable this function.

Snapping anchor points to grid intersections

You can also snap anchor points to grid intersections if Snap to Grid is enabled.

● With the Direct-selection tool active, select point. Click-drag to grid intersection.

Aligning objects into alignment with other objects

You can snap any part of an object into alignment with points and paths on another object with Smart Guides enabled.

   ① Click aligning point – anchor point, centre point or path segment – on object A to which you wish to align object B. The words anchor, centre or path will appear when the cursor moves over such objects.

   ② Click-drag aligning object B (you need not drag from an anchor or centre point on this object) to the aligning point on object A. Smart guides will appear.

   ③ Move the cursor up or down the guides until you are happy with the position of object B.

   ④ Release the mouse button.

Moving objects using the cursor keys

You can nudge objects into position with some accuracy using the cursor keys, provided the keyboard increment is set to a small amount.

Setting the keyboard increment

   ① Choose General from the Preferences sub-menu in the File menu. The General set of preferences will be displayed.

   ② Enter a value in the Cursor Key field (see Figure 8.1).

   ③ Click OK.

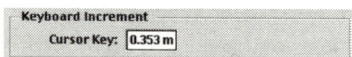

Figure 8.1 The Cursor Key field

Using the cursor keys

   ① Select the object(s) to be moved.

   ② Press ←, →, ↑ or ↓.

Moving objects using the Move command

The Move command lets you move an object (or a copy of an object) a specified distance and angle.

   ① With the Selection tool active, select object(s).

② Choose Move in the Transform sub-menu in the Object menu. The Move dialog box will be displayed (see Figure 8.2).

③ Enter values in the Distance and Angle fields.

④ Click OK or Copy.

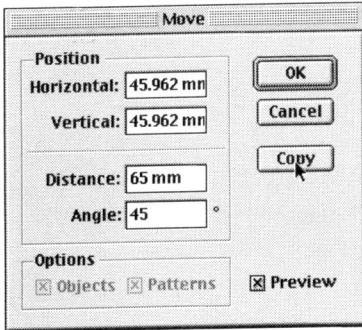

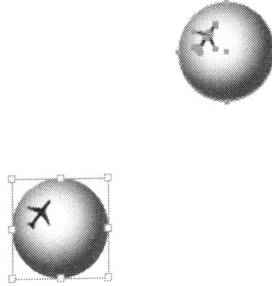

Figure 8.2 Moving a copy of an object a specified distance within the Move dialog box

You can set the distance and angle in this dialog box by using the Measure tool.

① Choose Info from the Window menu. The Info palette will be displayed (see Figure 8.3).

② With the Selection tool active, select an object or objects.

③ With the Measure tool active, click-drag from a point on the object(s) to another point on the artboard. Notice that the values for distance and angle are recorded in the Info palette. The same values will be entered into the Move dialog box when you next use the command.

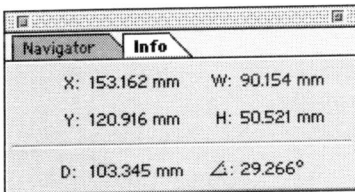

Figure 8.3 The Info palette showing the distance and angle recorded by the Measure tool

Moving objects using the Transform palette

This is the control to use for positioning objects to ruler coordinates.

① Choose Transform from the Window menu. The Transform palette will be displayed (see Figure 8.4).

② Select the object to be positioned.

③ Select the object point you wish to be located at the ruler coordinates. Do this by clicking one of nine points on the object proxy in the palette (it's to the left of the X and Y fields). Its eight anchor points and single centre point represent points on the selected object's bounding box.

④ Enter values in the X and Y fields.

⑤ Press [Enter ↵].

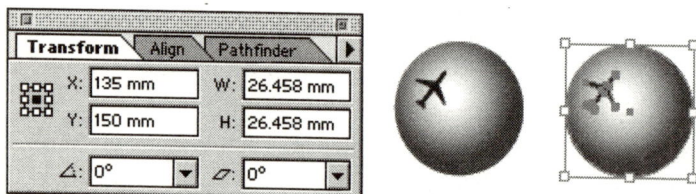

Figure 8.4 Moving a copy of an object to set coordinates using the Transform palette

Aligning and distributing items

You can accurately align and distribute items using the Align palette. You can align objects along a vertical axis, using the rightmost, centre or left-most points of selected objects, or along a horizontal axis, using the top-most, centre or bottommost points of selected objects. Furthermore you can distribute objects evenly along a vertical or horizontal axis or the space between objects evenly, both horizontally and vertically.

① With the Selection tool active, select more than one object.

② Choose Align from the Window menu. The Align palette will be displayed. Choose Show Options in the pop-up menu (press the triangle at the top right hand corner of the palette to access this menu) (see Figure 8.5).

③ Select an Align and/or Distribute option.

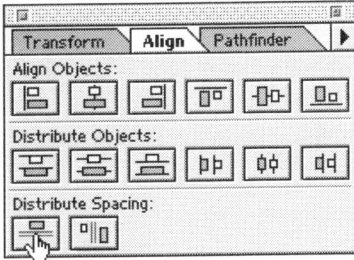

Figure 8.5 Distributing the spacing between objects

Setting new objects at an angle

New objects can be set to an angle other than the horizontal.

① Choose General... from the Preferences sub-menu in the File menu. The General set of preferences will be displayed.

② Under Tool behaviour (see Figure 8.6), enter a value in Constrain Angle field.

Figure 8.6 Setting the constrain angle for all new objects

! Remember to reset the control with a zero after you have finished creating angled objects.

Locking objects in position

Once objects are positioned correctly they can be locked on an object-by-object basis to prevent accidental movement through the use of the mouse.

① With the Selection tool active, select an item or items.

② Choose Lock from the Object menu (to tick the command).

▲ Objects can also be locked on a layer-by-layer basis (see page 93).

Unlocking objects

① Choose Unlock all from the Object menu. All object(s) on visible and/or unlocked layers will be unlocked.

Grouping objects together

Related objects can be grouped so that they act as a single entity while the Selection tool is active.

① With the Selection tool active, select the objects you wish to group.

② Choose Group from the Object menu.

▲ You can modify objects within a group with the Direct-selection tool active. You can group groups of objects if you wish. Use the Group-selection tool to select sub-groups (groups within groups).

Ungrouping objects

① With the Selection tool active, select an object within a group.

② Choose Ungroup from the Object menu.

Deleting objects

① With the appropriate Selection tool active, select an object or objects.

② Either: press [Delete] or: choose Clear from the Edit menu.

Applying other transformations to objects

Unlike editing operations covered elsewhere in this book, transformations affect the geometry of objects without changing their basic path structures. For instance, a square transformed into a parallelogram will have the same number of segments and intervening anchor points as it did before the transformation occurred.

Transformations are not restricted to objects. You can transform placed images and even type matter if you wish.

There are two ways to use the transform tools. Either you can use them in conjunction with the mouse or you can enter settings into dialog boxes. The former way allows you to view the objects as they are transforming, the latter way offers a more hands-off approach.

You can apply transformations using:

- the Selection tool
- the Free-transform tool
- the Transform palette
- one of the transform tools
- the transform commands

Resizing objects using their bounding boxes

Objects can simply be resized by applying the Selection tool to their bounding boxes, the rectangular boxes that encompass selected objects.

① With the Selection tool active, click within object(s) to be scaled. A rectangular bounding box will appear around the object(s).

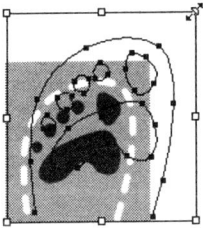

Figure 8.7 Scaling objects by click-dragging their boundary box

② Click-drag one of the handles of the edge of the bounding box (see Figure 8.7).

! The bounding box shows only if Use Bounding Box is selected within the General set of preferences.

▲ Pressing the Shift key during a scaling will maintain the proportion.

Transforming objects using the Free-transform tool

This tool lets you quickly scale, rotate, reflect, shear and distort objects in conjunction with modifier keys.

① Select the object(s) to be transformed.

② With the Free Transform tool active:

Click-drag handle of bounding box (not edge) to scale.

Click-drag edge of bounding box (not handle) to rotate.

Click-drag handle of bounding box (not edge) past the opposite edge or handle to reflect.

Click-drag edge of bounding box (not handle), and only then hold down [⌘] [Option], to shear.

Click-drag handle of bounding box (not edge), and only then hold down [⌘], to distort.

Transforming objects using the Transform palette

This palette is a veritable Swiss Army knife. You can use it to accurately resize, rotate and shear objects without resorting to other commands. Objects are resized not by percentages, as in the Scale dialog box, but by specifying a precise width and height.

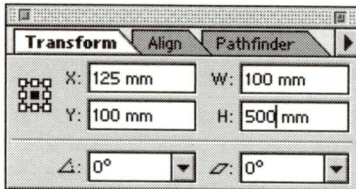

Figure 8.8 Resizing an object from its centre.

① Choose Transform from the Window menu. The Transform palette will be displayed (see Figure 8.8).

② Select object(s) to be scaled.

③ Select a point of origin on the object proxy.

④ Enter values in the W(idth) and H(eight) fields and/or choose a value from the Rotate and Shear pop-up menus.

⑤ Press [Enter ↵].

Using the transform tools

The transform tools provide a way to scale, rotate, reflect and shear objects from a designated point of origin by dragging the mouse or by setting values in dialog boxes.

To transform by setting values, select any one of the tools and [Option]+click within the artboard at the point from where you wish the transformation to originate. The relevant dialog box will be displayed.

Alternatively, if you are happy about transforming from a centre point, you can access the same controls in the Transform sub-menu.

By checking or ticking Preview in these boxes you can preview transformations before they are implemented and, by transforming copies of objects previously pasted in front of originals rather than copying objects within the dialog boxes themselves, you can preview effects against the originals.

Whether stroke weights, masked objects and patterned fills are transformed along with objects depends on the settings in these boxes.

Scaling objects

Scaling objects saves you having to redraw at different sizes and enables you to alter object proportions at will.

① Select the object(s) to be rotated.

② Select the Scale tool. Its point of origin will appear at the centre of the objects(s) you selected. If you wish to reposition the point, click anywhere within your artwork.

③ With the Scale tool still active, click-drag away or towards the point of origin. The further you drag, the greater the degree of enlargement or reduction.

▲ Holding down the Shift key during scaling will maintain object proportions. Holding down Alt when you reposition the point of origin will bring up the Scale dialog box (see Figure 8.9).

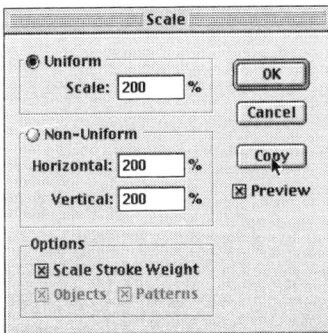

Figure 8.9 Scaling a copy of an object within the Scale dialog box. The point of origin was set at the centre of the motif

Rotating objects

Being able to rotate objects can save a great deal of time and enables you to create circular formations to a high degree of accuracy (see 125).

① Select the object(s) to be rotated.

② Select the Rotate tool. Its point of origin will appear at the centre of the objects(s) you selected. If you wish to reposition the point, click anywhere within your artwork.

③ With the Rotate tool still active, click-drag in an arc to rotate the object(s). The further the arc is away from the point of origin, the greater the degree of control.

▲ Holding down the Shift key during a drag will constrain rotations to 45° increments. Holding down Alt when you reposition the point of origin will bring up the Rotate dialog box (see Figure 8.10).

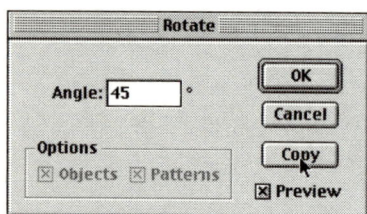

Figure 8.10 Rotating a copy of an object within the Rotate dialog box. The point of origin was set near the centre of the dart

Reflecting objects

Reflecting objects is the key to creating object symmetry. By reflecting a copy of the path representing one side of an object, you create a mirror image for the opposite side.

The process depends on positioning the reflect point of origin midway between the original object(s) and the object(s) to be reflected. This would be where you would imagine a small mirror to be. Once positioned you click-drag along the imaginary surface of this mirror to set the reflective angle.

① Select the object(s) to be reflected.

② Select the Reflect tool. Its point of origin will appear at the centre of the objects(s) you selected. Reposition the point by clicking at a midway point as described above.

③ With the Reflect tool still active, click-drag in an arc to alter the angle of reflection. The further the arc is away from the point of origin, the greater the degree of control.

▲ Holding down the Shift key during a reflection will constrain reflections to a vertical or horizontal axis. Holding down Alt when you reposition the point of origin will bring up the Reflect dialog box (see Figure 8.11).

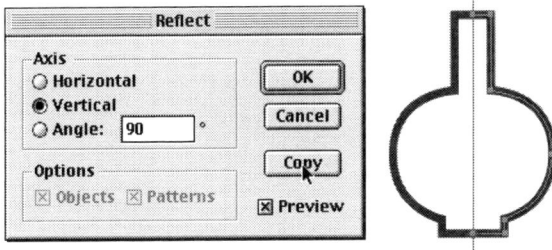

Figure 8.11 Reflecting a copy of an object profile within the Reflect dialog box. The point of origin was set where the two bottom end points meet

Shearing objects

Shearing an object makes it appear that the plane the object is resting on has been rotated. It is therefore ideal for creating perspective and axonometric effects in drawings, the latter often achieved in conjunction with the Scale tool which is applied first.

Shearing can take some getting used to as it's easy to shear the wrong way. Contrary to what you might think, vertical settings affect horizontal lines in an object and horizontal settings vertical lines. Angle settings add to the equation by rotating the sheared result.

① Select the object(s) to be sheared.

② Select the Shear tool. Its point of origin will appear at the centre of the objects(s) you selected. If you wish to reposition the point, click anywhere within your artwork.

③ With the Shear tool still active, click-drag one edge of the object. The further you drag, the greater the degree of shear.

▲ Holding down the Shift key during a drag will prevent a shear from distorting. Holding down Alt when you reposition the point of origin will bring up the Shear dialog box (see Figure 8.12).

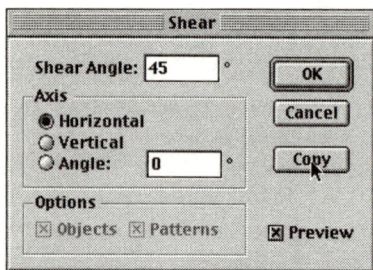

Figure 8.12 Shearing a copy of an object within the Shear dialog box. The point of origin was set at the base of the building

Duplicating objects

Duplication commands control copies of single and multiple objects.

You can duplicate objects by:

- direct copying
- copying and pasting
- repeating a transformation
- stepping and repeating.

Direct copying

Direct copying simply involves using the Alt key in conjunction with the mouse. This is the quickest way to copy objects.

① With the appropriate Selection tool active, select object(s).

② Hold down [Option] and click-drag. An outlined copy of the objects(s) will appear under a double-arrowed cursor.

▲ Press Command (Control)-Alt to save switching to a selection tool.

Copying and pasting

This process involves the use of the clipboard (a short-term storage area assigned for this purpose). Any object you copy is automatically placed on the clipboard. Any object you paste will be placed in the middle of the viewing area unless you use the Paste in Front or Paste at Back routine (see Altering the stacking within layers, page 95).

However many times you paste, the object will remain on the clipboard until another object is copied.

① Select the whole artwork or the part of the artwork you wish to copy, by using one of the selection methods described in Chapter 7. Choose Copy in the Edit menu (or press ⌘+A).

② If you wish to paste within another document, move to that document. Otherwise skip this step.

③ Select the layer on which you wish to paste the objects on the clipboard.

④ Choose Paste in the Edit menu (or press ⌘+V). The copy will be pasted on the active layer.

⑤ Reposition the image, as necessary.

Repeating a transformation

The Transform Again command lets you repeat the last transformation, however complex. If the original transformation involved copying, transformed copies will be made of objects.

① Make a transformation.

② Choose Transform Again from the Transform sub-menu in the Object menu.

Stepping and repeating

You can easily create repeat images in Illustrator using the Move and Transform Again commands. The process involves moving copies of objects at specified distances from each other and to a specified angle.

① With the Selection tool active, select an item or items.

② Choose Move in the Transform sub-menu in the Object menu. The Move dialog box will be displayed (see Figure 8.13).

③ Enter values in the Distance and Angle fields.

④ Click Copy.

⑤ Choose Transform Again from the Transform sub-menu in the Object menu.

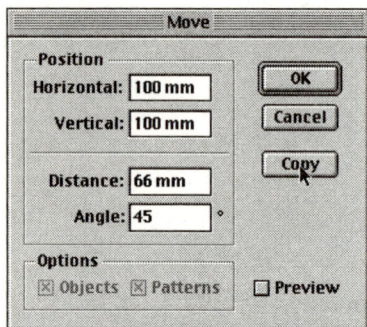

Figure 8.13 Moving an object by specifying a distance and angle

▲ You can also create multiple effects using patterns, see page 127.

Summary

Repositioning objects Objects are repositioned by either using the mouse, the cursor keys, the Move command, the Transform palette or the Align palette.

Repositioning methods The Move command moves objects by specified distances, the Transform palette to artwork coordinates and the Align palette into spatial relationships with other objects.

Transforming objects Objects can be transformed from their centres or from a designated point of origin, subject to the method employed.

Repeating objects Objects can be repeated by direct copying, copying and pasting and by stepping and repeating.

9 | USING SPECIAL TECHNIQUES

Objects from objects

The forms of most manufactured items are made up of simple shapes, rectangles, ellipses, segments and such like. The same is true for some natural objects. So when you are drawing in Illustrator look for the simple shapes that make up items and start off with objects representing these shapes. You can then use one of the Pathfinder commands to merge or divide the objects to create the shapes you really require (see Figure 9.2).

Whether you use these automated commands or operate on objects manually, creating complex shapes from objects that are more easily drawn saves time and is generally more accurate.

In earlier versions of Illustrator operating on objects involved spending a lot of time cutting and joining paths using the Pen and Scissors tools.

It was not unlike working in an operating theatre except it wasn't a matter of life or death. The work was detailed, painstaking and nerve wracking. A single incorrect move of the cursor could mean starting all over again. With the Pathfinder commands such work is now stress-free.

Editing using the Pathfinder palette

① Choose Pathfinder from the Window palette. The Pathfinder palette will be displayed (see Figure 9.1).

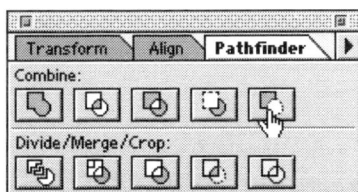

Figure 9.1 The Pathfinder palette

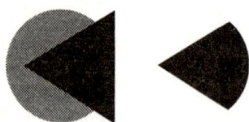

Intersect removes non-overlapping areas

Exclude does the opposite of Intersect

Minus Front knocks front objects out of back objects

Minus Back does the opposite of Minus Front

Divide creates objects from previously overlapping and non-overlapping areas

Unite does the opposite of Divide by creating one object from previously separate objects

Trim removes hidden parts of filled paths

Merge does the same as Trim but merges overlapping objects with the same fill

Figure 9.2 Key Pathfinder operations: some of the results have been exploded for clarity

② With the Selection tool active, select the objects you wish to edit.

③ Click one of the Pathfinder buttons.

The Pathfinder functions and what they do

Unite joins multiple objects together as one object.

Intersect creates objects from overlapping areas.

Exclude creates objects excluding overlapping areas.

Minus Front takes the area of a front object away from a back object.

Minus Back takes the area of a back object away from a front object.

Divide breaks up objects into previously non-overlapping and overlapping areas.

Trim removes areas of a back object underlapping a front object.

Merge knocks out the underlapping area of the back object.

Crop uses the front object as a cropping area for the back object.

Outline removes fills from objects and divides paths.

Distorted lines

You can distort object paths in various ways using special effect filters including Punk and Bloat, Roughen, Scribble and Tweak, Twirl and Zigzag (see Figure 9.3).

The Punk and Bloat filter curves objects inward and outward from their anchor points and the Roughen filter moves anchor points in a jagged array to give objects rough edges. The Scribble and Tweak filter distorts objects in different ways; Scribble moves anchor points away from objects, Tweak moves them in the direction of your choice. The Twirl filter in conjunction with the Twirl tool rotates objects more sharply at their centres than at their edges. And the Zigzag filter? Well, it creates zigzags!

Previewing and applying effects

① With the Selection tool active, select an object.

② Choose a filter from the Distort sub-menu in the Filter menu. The appropriate dialog box will be displayed.

③ Enter values and select options.

④ Check or tick Preview to preview the effect.

⑤ Click OK to apply the filter.

Figure 9.3 Distort effects clockwise from top left: original, Punk and Bloat, Roughen, Scribble and Tweak, Twirl, Zigzag

Holes in objects

Transparent areas are required in many types of artwork object, not least logos and most types of letterform, as objects need to show through their interior spaces. Such transparency is achieved by a process called 'compounding' which effectively creates holes where objects overlap. It's simple to do and relies for its success on the alternation of path directions.

Figure 9.4 Distorted rectangle and pointed oval are compounded to give the effect of a hole

Compounding objects

① With the Selection tool active, select two or more overlapping, ungrouped and unlocked closed paths.

② Choose Make from the Compound Paths sub-menu in the Object menu.

The overlapping areas of the objects should now be transparent (see Figure 9.4). Should they not be, you need to manually reverse the direction of one or more of the paths.

Reversing the direction of paths

All paths have a direction associated with them. This is determined by the order you plot paths or, in the case of objects created using the simple shape tools, how Illustrator plots paths. It's often academic whether a closed path has a clockwise or anticlockwise direction as this attribute can't be seen. However, for compounding to work, path directions need to alternate between the two directions – and if they don't they need to be made to do so (see Figure 9.5).

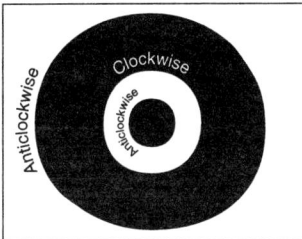

Figure 9.5 Alternating path directions within compounded objects

① Choose Attributes from the Window menu. The Attributes palette will be displayed.

② With the Direct-selection tool active, select one of the paths.

③ Click the Reverse Path Direction On button (see Figure 9.6).

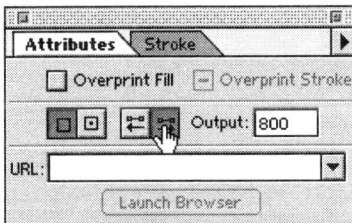

Figure 9.6 Reversing the direction of a path

Releasing compounding objects

This command returns objects to their non-compounded state. Holes and other attributes of compounding will disappear.

① With the Selection tool active, select the compounded objects.

② Choose Release from the Compound Paths sub-menu in the Object menu.

Running fills across objects

As compounded objects behave as single objects, the process allows you not only to create holes but also to run a single colour, gradient or patterned fill across its solid areas, whatever their position in your artwork (see Figure 9.7). If any of the objects overlap holes will appear – unless, of course, you reverse path directions.

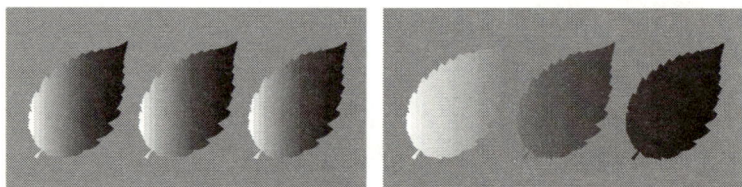

Figure 9.7 The same gradient fill before (left) and after compounding (right)

Positive/negative effects

The solid and transparent areas created through compounding can be exploited for their positive/negative appearance (see Figure 9.8). The process is the same as for creating holes; it's just a difference of intent.

Figure 9.8 Positive/negative effect in logo

Modelling, gradients and tweening

Whilst Illustrator objects are unavoidably hard-edged this doesn't mean they can't be finely modelled. It's just a question of applying the right graduation effect to particular object areas.

Modelling is achieved using the Gradient, Blend or Mesh tools. Success in using these tools for modelling purposes relies very much on an understanding of structures and the way that light falls on surfaces. However you don't need specialist knowledge to create simple effects or to use the Blend tool to 'tween' objects. You just need imagination!

Blending colours

Elsewhere in this book I have discussed how to create graduated effects using the Gradient palette. Here we look at how to create graduations using the Blend tool.

Blends are superior to gradient fills for a number of reasons:

- they are not restricted to linear or radial forms
- they can be less prone to banding
- they generally output faster
- they can be trapped.

Blending involves creating shapes from many small objects and assigning each a different fill. The eye blends the fills together to give a continuous tonal effect (see Figure 9.9).

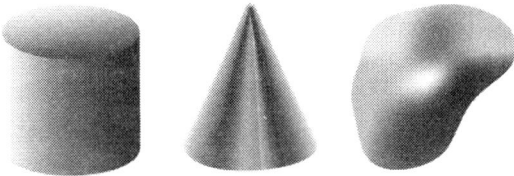

Figure 9.9 Tones rendered by a gradient fill (left), by blended objects (centre) and by a gradient mesh (right)

Illustrator automatically creates the intermediate objects for you. All you need to do is create suitably filled objects for the start and finish of a blend and let the program do the rest.

Having said this, it's crucial that the shapes of the objects and their orientation in the blend are correct as both factors determine not only the shape of a blend but its overall character.

A completed blend is controlled by a path connecting all objects. If you plan to curve the path after a blend is made Align to Path will orient its objects at right angles to the centre line of blend whereas Align to Page will not affect their orientation.

The number of intermediate objects generated by the blend is also important, especially if smooth transitions are to be attained. Smooth Colour creates an optimum number of blend objects based on the difference between the starting and finishing colours. This may not result in enough blend objects to span the distance, in which case a Specified Steps setting will be required (see Printing gradients, page 187).

Creating a wavy blend

① Create a wavy shape where you wish the gradient to begin.

② Duplicate the shape and position it where you wish the gradient to end.

③ Assign each object a different colour.

④ For the purpose of this exercise, assign each object a None stroke.

⑤ With the Blend tool active, hold down ⌥Option and click in the centre of the first shape. The Blend Options dialog box will be displayed (see Figure 9.10).

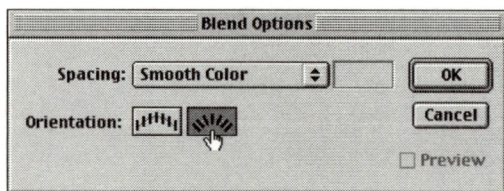

Figure 9.10 The Blend Options dialog box with Align to Path selected

⑥ Choose either Smooth Colour or Specified steps from the Spacing pop-up menu.

⑦ Select an option under Orientation.

⑧ Click OK.

⑨ With the Blend tool still active click in the centre of the second shape. Intermediate objects are automatically generated with different fill colours (see Figure 9.11).

Altering blend colours

① With the Direct-selection tool active, select the first object

② Assign the object a different colour.

③ Repeat steps 1 and 2 for the last object.

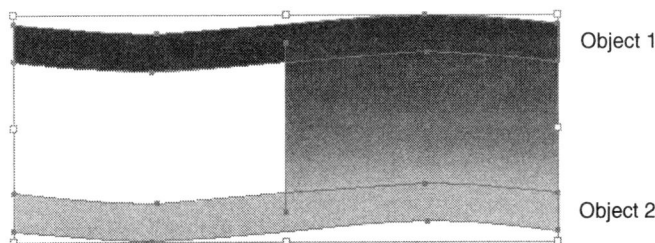

Figure 9.11 Split image: two wavy shapes selected for blending (left side) and the resultant blend (right side)

Altering blend options

① Choose Blend Options from the Blend menu in the Object menu.

② Alter settings as required.

③ Click OK.

Amending the shape of blends

① With the Direct-selection tool active, select the path running down the centre of the blend.

② Alter path as required, adding and manipulating anchor points as necessary.

Meshing colours

If you wish to mix several gradients within a single enclosed path you can do so using the Gradient Mesh tool or command.

Both enable you to create multi-coloured objects in which colours can flow in different directions graduating from one point to another. The process involves creating a mesh on an object and applying colour to its intersecting points and/or enclosed areas.

In a sense meshing objects combines aspects of both blending and gradient fills with its use of multiple areas and colour transitions.

When a mesh object is created multiple lines crisscross its internal area. By moving and editing points on these lines you can change the intensity of a colour shift or the extent of a coloured area. At the intersection of these mesh lines are special diamond-shaped anchor points called mesh points.

These behave as ordinary anchor points, except they accept colour and cannot be deleted. The area between four mesh points is called a mesh patch. You can change the colour of a mesh patch using the same techniques as changing colours in a mesh point.

It's worth bearing in mind the following when creating mesh objects:

- You cannot create mesh objects from compound paths, text objects or placed EPS files.
- The Gradient Mesh command works best when converting complex objects.
- The Gradient Mesh command creates a regular pattern of mesh points.
- The Gradient Mesh tool is good for creating points where you wish a highlight to appear.
- A number of small simple mesh objects is preferred to a single large complex object from the point of view of fast screen redraw.
- You cannot convert a mesh object back to a normal path object.

Creating a mesh object using the Gradient Mesh command

① With the selection tool active, create a filled object.

② Choose Create Gradient Mesh from the Object menu. The Create Gradient Mesh dialog box will be displayed (see Figure 9.12).

③ Enter the number of horizontal rows of mesh lines in the Rows field.

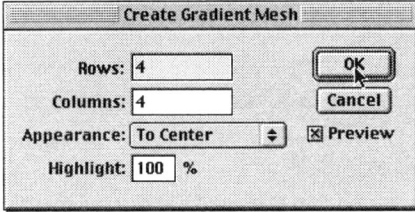

Figure 9.12 The Create Gradient Mesh dialog box

④ Enter the number of vertical columns of mesh lines in the Columns field.

⑤ Choose an option from the Appearance pop-up menu. To Centre creates a highlight in the centre of an object. To Edge creates a highlight at the edges of an object. Flat results in no highlight

⑥ Enter a percentage of white highlight to apply to the mesh object. 100% gives a full white highlight, 0% gives no white highlight.

⑦ Click OK.

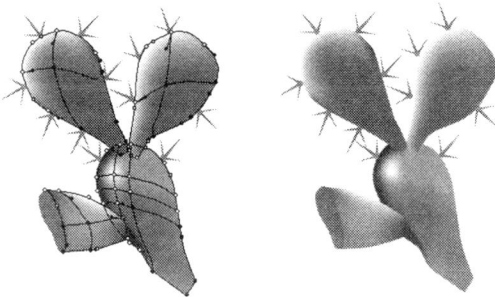

Figure 9.13 Cactus with and without mesh selected

Creating a mesh object using the Gradient Mesh tool

① With the selection tool active, create a filled object.

② With the Gradient Mesh tool active, click within object. The object is converted to a gradient mesh object with the minimum number of mesh patches (see Figure 9.13).

③ Click within mesh patches to create further mesh patches.

Colouring a mesh object

① With the Gradient Mesh or Direct-selection tool active

Either: click on mesh point if you wish to apply colour around single point.

Or: within mesh patch if you wish to colour around all four mesh points.

② Choose a colour in the normal manner.

Tweening shapes

Blending is not only useful for graduating colours, it's also a superb tool for tweening – creating a few intermediate shapes between two or more drawn objects (see Figure 9.14).

Creating intermediate objects

① Create three objects with flat fills.

② For the purpose of this exercise, assign each object a None stroke.

③ With the Blend tool active, click in the centre of each shape. Hold down [Option] when you click on last shape. The Blend Options dialog box will be displayed (see Figure 9.10).

④ Choose Specified Steps in the Spacing pop-up menu.

⑤ Enter 1 in the field to the right of the menu.

⑥ Click Align to Path if you wish the blend objects to run at right angle to centre line of new blend. Otherwise click Align to Page.

⑦ Click OK.

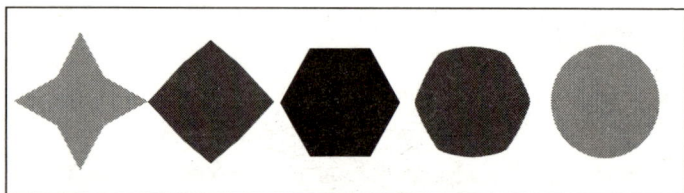

Figure 9.14 The second and fourth objects from the left are tweened from the other objects

⑧ With the Blend tool still active click in the centre of the second and third objects. A single tweened object will be generated between the three original objects.

Double lines, outlines and shapes

Creating double lines

Double lines may not be the most exciting of graphic items but I include them here as they are often required in artworks yet are difficult to create if you don't use the correct method.

They are to be found in all sorts of maps and diagrams to denote lines of communication, flowlines, arteries and such like. The difficulty arises out of the need to keep the lines at a constant gauge. If you create them side by side you will find it impossible to keep them a set distance apart.

The answer lies in superimposing the paths and giving them a different width and colour. All you then have to worry about is ensuring that the two paths remain superimposed (see Figure 9.15). This can be simply done by locking them in place.

Creating roads

① Create a layer and name it 'Road Outline'.

② On this layer, create a series of paths representing the road system.

③ Set their stroke width to 10 pt, their stroke colour to black and set their fill to None.

④ Duplicate layer and name it 'Road Inline'.

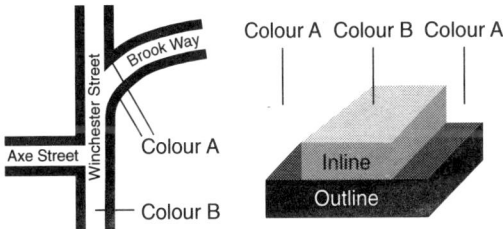

Figure 9.15 A road system composed of overlapping paths

⑤ Select the objects on the new layer ('Road Inline") and set their stroke width to 6 pt and their stroke colour to white, maintaining the Transparent fill. The wider black stroke on 'Road Outline' layer will appear either side of the narrower white stroke on 'Road Inline' layer to give a double-line effect.

Outlining objects

Elsewhere in this book I have discussed how to change the caps and joins of strokes. Here I discuss this aspect in the context of butted objects (see next section) as this is where stroking is most problematic. Problematic because butted objects imply superimposed paths where strokes can overshoot and look unresolved at path junctions (see Figure 9.16).

Sometimes it can be resolved by selecting different end caps and corner joins in various combinations. However, on large objects it's sometimes necessary to resort to converting strokes to closed paths and adjusting their edges until path alignments are spot on.

Figure 9.16 Stroke of grey object (left) converted to outlines and re-adjusted (right)

Converting a stroke into a closed path

① With the Selection tool active, select any number of objects, either stroked or unstroked.

② Choose Outline Path from the Path sub-menu in the object menu. All stroked paths will be replaced by enclosed paths set to a None stroke.

③ Edit the paths as required.

Creating butted shapes

You can create butted effects in simple artworks by just overlapping objects. But where many shapes are involved it's necessary for each to be correctly shaped so that they can butt together at their edges. Maps are a good example as districts and regions, represented by tonal or coloured areas, need to fit together with a degree of accuracy. The butting technique involves the accurate trimming of objects or, to be more precise, closed paths (see Figure 9.17).

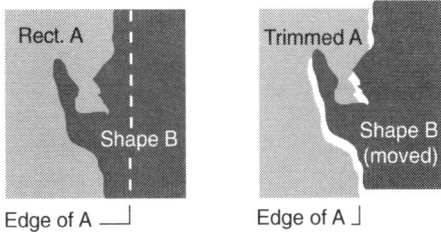

Figure 9.17 Rectangle A trimmed back by shape B (moved for clarity)

① Create a layer and name it 'Districts'.

② On this layer, create two shapes representing adjacent urban areas. Draw the first shape accurately. Where the second shape abuts the first shape run it slightly over its border.

③ Send the second shape behind the first shape.

④ Set both stroke widths to 0 pt but give them different-coloured fills.

⑤ Select both objects.

⑥ Choose Pathfinder from the Window menu. The Pathfinder palette will be displayed.

⑦ Under Divide/Merge/Crop, click Trim. The lower item will be trimmed back to the top item's border.

⑧ Choose Ungroup from the Object menu to ungroup both objects.

⑨ Choose Lock from the Object menu to lock both objects.

Formations and repeats

Creating circular formations

Clockfaces, dials, cogs, flower heads; all these items share a common structure. In plan view they are circular in formation with items – numerals, teeth, etc. – equally spaced around their periphery. Positioning these items accurately around a centre point involves the use of guides and ellipses and the deft use of the Rotate tool and Repeat Transform command.

① With the Ellipse tool active, create a large circle.

② Choose Make Guides from the View menu to turn the circle into an object guide.

③ Create vertical and horizontal ruler guides to align with the centre of the circular guide.

④ With the Type tool active, type the numeral '1' within and just touching the topmost edge of the circular guide. Centre align the 1 in the paragraph palette and reposition it if necessary.

⑤ With the Rotate tool active, press ⌥Option and click the centre of the circular guide. The Rotate dialog box will be displayed (see Figure 9.18).

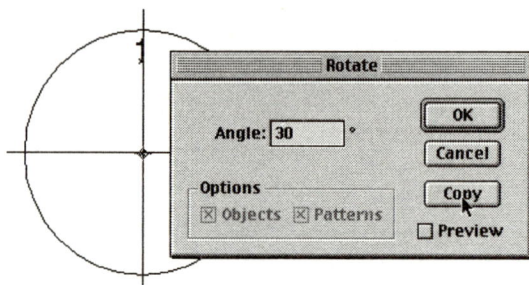

Figure 9.18 Rotating a copy of an object around the point of origin

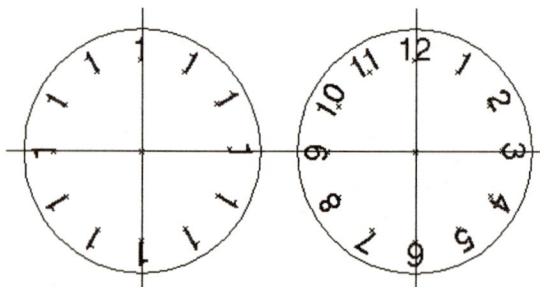

Figure 9.19 The repeated numerals (left) reset with the correct numerals (right)

⑥ Enter 30 in the Angle field.

⑦ Click Copy. A copy of the circle will be placed within the circular guide.

⑧ Choose Transform Again in the Transform sub-menu of the Object menu or press ⌘+[D]. Repeat nine times to give you a further nine figures (see Figure 9.19).

Creating repeat designs

Two types of design repeat can be created within Illustrator. You can create tile patterns for filling objects and brush patterns for stroking paths. Here we look at how a tile pattern is created, applied and transformed.

One essential component of a tile artwork is its bounding object. This object must be a rectangle and should encompass all the other objects, even if it's rendered invisible by having no fill and stroke. It also must be behind all the other objects.

Bear in mind when you are creating your own designs that both types of repeat are object-rich so it's best to keep designs as simple as possible to avoid memory and outputting problems (see Figure 9.20).

Creating a tile pattern

① Create a design using a series of objects.

② Using the Rectangle tool, create a rectangle and send it behind the other objects. This rectangle will act as a bounding box to your design.

③ With the Select tool active, select all the objects, including the rectangle.

Figure 9.20 A tile design comprising a coloured square and flower motif (left). The same design applied to a rectangle (right)

④ Enter a name for the swatch in the Swatch Name field.

⑤ Choose Define Pattern... from the Edit menu. The New Swatch dialog box will be displayed (see Figure 9.21).

⑥ Click OK. The pattern will automatically be added to the Swatches palette.

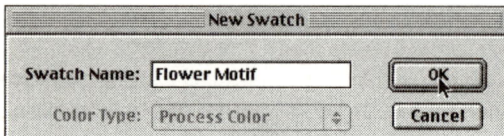

Figure 9.21 Naming a new pattern swatch

Applying pattern fills

① Select Show Swatches from the Window menu.

② Select the object(s) to be patterned.

③ Click once in the fill box in the toolbox (if the box is already overlapping there is no need to click).

④ Click a pattern within the Swatches palette.

▲ Remove a patterned fill by just selecting another fill.

Transforming objects with patterned fills

When you transform patterned objects, the pattern fill can transform with the object or not, depending on the current dialog box settings. To alter these settings:

① Double-click on a transform tool in the toolbox, such as the Scale tool. Its dialog box will be displayed.

② Under Options, Check/uncheck or tick/untick Patterns (see Figure 9.22).

③ Click OK.

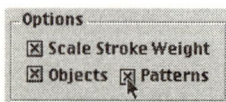

Figure 9.22 The Patterns option in the Scale dialog box

Colour on colour and masks

Colour on colour

You can simulate the blending effect of overprinted colours by using the Hard or Soft Mix filters. You can, of course, truly overprint colours by specifying overprinting in the Attributes palette. However, the latter feature is implemented only during imagesetting; it's the less versatile and predictable of the two methods.

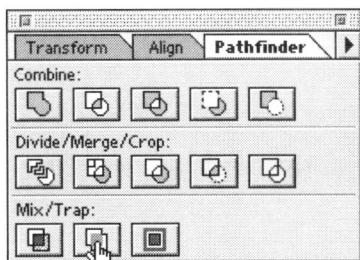

Figure 9.23 Applying a soft mix to overlapping paper shapes

To create an overlay effect

① Create two closed paths, each with a different fill colour.

② Overlap the two paths.

③ With the selection tool active, select the two paths.

④ Choose Pathfinder from the Window menu. The Pathfinder palette will be displayed (see Figure 9.23). Choose Show Options in the pop-up menu (press the triangle at the top right hand corner of the palette to access this menu).

⑤ Click Hard or Soft Mix.

! In the process objects will be automatically grouped. If you wish to perform further colour overlay experiments with these objects you will need to ungroup them by pressing Command (Control)-Shift+G.

Masking objects

You can mask out – clip – areas of an artwork within Illustrator to hide unresolved edges, trap objects against multiple backgrounds or to crop placed images (see Figure 9.24)

To mask objects

① Create or position the closed path you wish to use as a mask over the object(s) to be masked.

Figure 9.24 Unmasked image (left). Same image masked by closed path (right)

② With the Selection tool active, select all objects (including the mask object).

③ Choose Make from the Mask sub-menu in the Object menu. Those parts of the objects outside the overlaying masking object will be hidden from view.

To release mask contents

① With the Selection tool active, select the masking object.

② Choose Release from the Mask sub-menu in the Object menu.

Summary

Operations The Pathfinder palette facilitates the operation of complex editing work on objects.

Creating transparency Transparency is achieved by compounding.

Blending colours Object-based gradients and 'tweening' are achieved using the Blend tool.

Maps Lines of communication, and regions, are easily created by stacking paths and by using the Trim Pathfinder.

Multiple transformations The Rotate command is useful for placing objects in a circular formation.

Repeats Designs can be assigned as patterns for repeated use within objects.

Masks Untidy areas and backgrounds can be clipped using masks.

10 | CREATING GRAPHS

Graphs in Illustrator

Graphs give visual expression to abstract data which cannot effectively be depicted by other means.

In Illustrator graphs can be created using its graph tools and controls. Whilst these automate the production process the results are effective only if their data is appropriate for the graph type.

Using the automated tools rather than 'hand-crafting' graphs saves time but the results, if unmodified, can look run-of-the-mill. Fortunately, graph components can be modified at will to meet your creative needs.

There are nine standard graph types available to you:

- Column and stacked column
- Bar and stacked bar
- Line and area
- Scatter
- Pie
- Radar

Graphs created by Illustrator's graphing tools are composed of grouped objects. Whilst they are maintained as groups, their data and appearance can be modified using the graph dialog boxes. When ungrouped, however, graph objects can be altered only manually.

Graph tools and controls

The relationship and functions of the graphing controls is not obvious at first glance. It is only through repeated use that you will choose the right one for a particular control function first time round.

The dialog box functions

Graph dimensions can be entered into the Graph dialog box when you *first* create a graph. However, you cannot later access the dialog box to resize graphs.

Graph data is always entered into the Data palette. This is automatically displayed when you create a graph using any one of the graph tools. You can access this palette at any time to update graph data.

Graph types, such as stacked column or pie, are initially determined by the graph tool you use to create a graph. Once a graph is created you can switch graph types at any time within the Type dialog box. Values are repositioned in the Value Axis pop-up menu in the same dialog box.

Custom graph designs (graph column and marker designs of your own making) are assigned as designs within the Design dialog box. They are selected within the Column dialog box to substitute for standard columns and within the Marker dialog box to substitute for standard markers (in line or scatter graphs).

Creating graphs

Creating standard graphs

①With one of the graph tools selected

Either: click-drag diagonally to define the dimensions and position of the graph.

Or: click on the artboard. The Graph dialog box will be displayed (see Figure 10.1). Enter values in the Width and Height fields. Click OK. The Graph Data dialog box will then be displayed (see Figure 10.2).

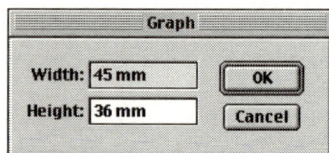

	Graph	
Width:	45 mm	OK
Height:	36 mm	Cancel

Figure 10.1 Overall graph dimensions can be entered in the Graph dialog box

② Enter data into this miniature spreadsheet by typing, cutting and pasting or importing.

Figure 10.2 Entering graph data

Text entered into column headings (in Figure 10.2, the city names) will act as legends in completed graphs. Each heading – or label – describes the column of data (data series) beneath it.

Text entered to the left of rows – row labels (in Figure 10.2, the years) – categorize data in each row, depending on the type of graph you have chosen.

③ Click the Tick icon or press [Enter ↵] to see the effect (see Figure 10.3).

④ Close the dialog box.

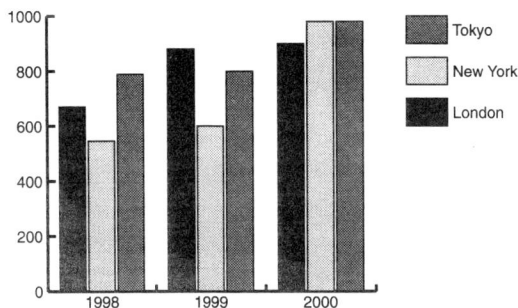

Figure 10.3 A standard column graph without modifications

▲ Use a | (vertical slash), instead of Shift-Return, to break lines within labels. Note that numbered labels, such as 2000, must be set in double quotes.

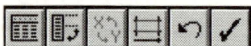

Figure 10.4 Graph Data dialog buttons. From left to right: Import data, Transpose row/column, Switch x/y, Cell style, Revert, Apply

Entering data using the keyboard

① Click in the first row of the second column (Figure 10.2 is used here as a example). The Entry line at the top left of the dialog box will be ready to take data for this cell.

② Enter a column label, such as London.

③ Click in the second row of the first column. The Entry line will be ready to take data for this cell.

④ Enter a row label, such as "1998".

⑤ Click in the second row of the second column. The Entry line will be ready to take data for this cell.

⑥ Enter data, such as 670.

⑦ Complete all the entries in this manner.

Entering data by copying and pasting

Data can be copied directly from a spreadsheet or word processed document, provided it contains no commas.

① Click in the top-left cell. The Entry line will be ready to take data for this cell.

② Paste data copied from cells or tabbed text.

Entering data by importing

Data can be imported provided it is formatted as tabbed text.

① Click in the top-left cell. The Entry line will be ready to take data for this cell.

② Click the Import data icon (see Figure 10.4). A directory dialog box will be displayed. Locate and open the text file to be imported.

③ Click Open.

Transposing labels

● Click the Transpose row/column button to switch the labels.

Transposing axes in scatter graphs

● Click the Switch x/y button to switch the axes in scatter graphs.

Adjusting cell widths

● Click-drag the edge of the column.

Entering labels and data to suit graph types

Column and stacked column

Enter numbers along y axis and data labels along x axis.

Bar and stacked bar

Enter numbers along x axis and data labels along y axis.

Column and stacked column, bar and stacked bar

For column and bar types you can combine positive and negative values. For stacked column and bar types values must be all positive.

Line

Enter numbers representing time along the x axis and numbers representing quantities along the y axis. Each column corresponds to one line in the graph. Positive and negative values can be combined.

Area

Each row of data corresponds to a filled area on the graph. Area graphs add each column's values to the previous column's totals. Only positive values can be included.

Scatter

Enter x axis data in first column and y axis data in second column. Any labels will be ignored.

Pie

Enter only one row of data, either all positive or all negative. Extra rows of data create separate graphs.

Radar

Enter data labels in first column and sets of numbers in each successive column. Each row represents a separate axis, of which you can have more than two.

Altering graphs

Altering the type of graph

① Select Type... from the Graphs sub-menu in the Object menu. The Graph Type dialog box will be displayed (see Figure 10.5).

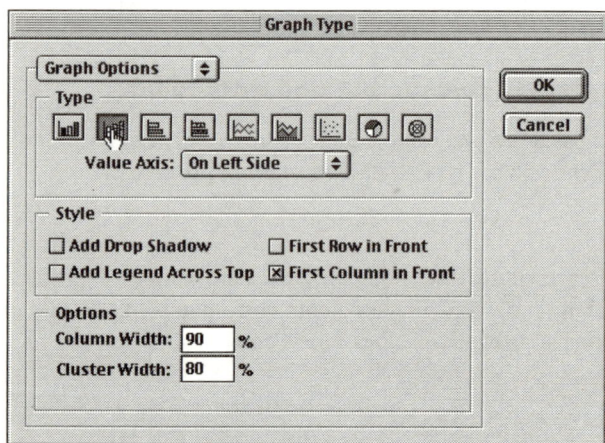

Figure 10.5 Altering a graph type to a stacked column

② Select an option in Type, such as Stacked column.

③ Click OK.

Colouring graph legends and columns

① With the Group-selection tool active, double or treble-click the first legend of the graph to select both legend and related column(s).

② Alter the fill and stroke of the objects in the normal way.

Altering graph data

① With the Selection tool active, select the graph.

② Select Data… from the Graphs sub-menu in the Object menu. The Data dialog box will be displayed.

③ Amend the data as required.

④ Press Enter to see the changes.

⑤ Close the dialog box.

Creating your own custom column

It's not possible in this section to cover all possible options. Therefore the following is limited to showing how a column artwork is produced and incorporated into a standard column graph (see Figure 10.6). If your particular need is not covered, you might at least be able to gain an understanding of general principles from this one example.

Phase one: creating a column artwork

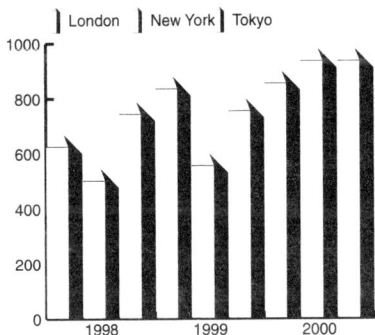

Figure 10.6 Graph with a custom column design

① Draw a design. In Figure 10.7 we show a simple skyscraper shape.

② Using the Rectangle tool, create a rectangle over the design, so it encompasses all the objects. Specify no fill or stroke and send it behind the other objects. This rectangle will act as an invisible bounding box to your design.

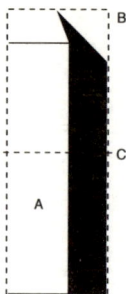

Figure 10.7 Column design (A) is bounded by rectangle (B) and crossed by guide (C)

③ Use the Pen tool to draw a horizontal line to define where the design will be extended or compressed. This line should extend right across the design and be slightly wider than the bounding box. It's only necessary to complete this step if you wish your design to telescope from a fixed point.

④ Select all parts of the artwork, including the horizontal line, and choose Group from the Object menu.

⑤ Select the horizontal line only, with the Direct-selection tool active, and choose Make from the Guides sub-menu in the Object menu. It's only necessary to complete this step if you completed step 3.

⑥ Choose Lock Guides from the Object menu (to untick the command).

Phase two: copying and painting column artworks

① With the Selection tool active, reselect the whole column artwork. Make several copies of the artwork, one for each proposed column label.

② Deselect the first artwork, including its bounding rectangle.

③ With the Direct-selection tool active, select and paint each artwork object in turn, excluding their bounding rectangles.

④ Repeat steps 2 and 3 for each copy of the artwork.

Phase three: assigning artworks as column designs

① With the Selection tool active, reselect one copy of the artwork.

② Choose Design... from the Graphs sub-menu in the Object menu. The Graph Design dialog box will be displayed (see Figure 10.8).

③ Click New Design. The design will be listed and shown in the Preview window.

④ Click Rename and enter a name in the Name field.

⑤ Click OK to return to the Graph Design dialog box. Then click OK again.

⑥ Repeat the steps for each copy of the artwork.

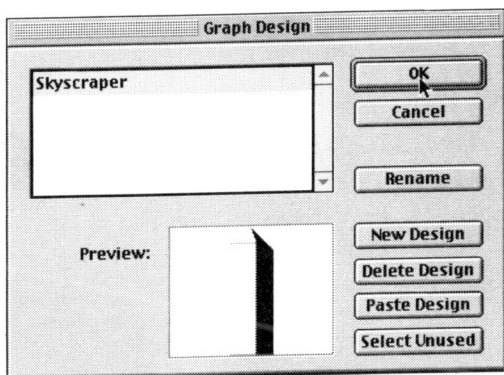

Figure 10.8 Assigning a column artwork as a graph design

Phase four: incorporating column designs in graphs

① With the Group-selection tool active, double or treble-click the top legend of your graph to select the legend and related columns.

② Choose Column... from the Graphs sub-menu in the Object menu. The Graph Column dialog box will be displayed (see Figure 10.9).

③ Under Choose Column Design, select one of the named designs. Choose an option in the Column Type pop-up menu. If your column design includes a horizontal guide, you have the option of choosing Sliding. Uncheck or untick Rotate Legend Design.

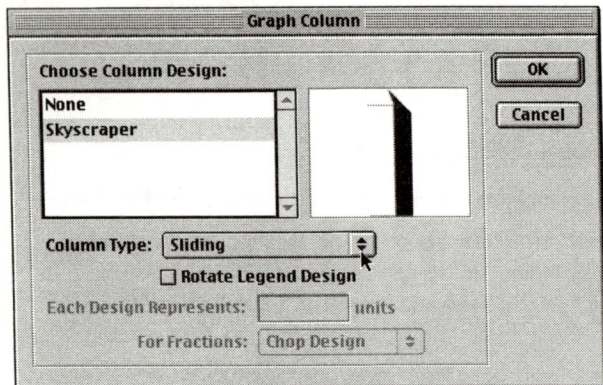

Figure 10.9 Incorporating a column design into a graph

Phase five: altering the stacking order of columns

① With the Selection tool active, select the whole graph.

② Select Type… from the Graphs sub-menu in the Object menu. The Graph Type dialog box will be displayed (see Figure 10.10).

③ Check or tick First Column in Front.

④ Click OK.

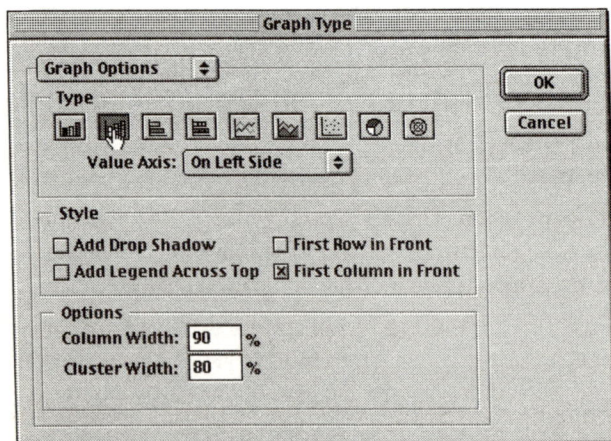

Figure 10.10 Specifying the first column to be in front

Creating your own custom marker

The process of creating a custom marker is not dissimilar to that of creating a custom column.

Phase one: creating a marker artwork

① Create a square, without fill and stroke, as the backmost object of the design. This acts as an invisible bounding box.

② Draw a design in front of and just within the square. In Figure 10.11 we show a simple globe with aircraft shadow within the square.

③ With the Selection tool active, select and paint each artwork object in turn, excluding the bounding square.

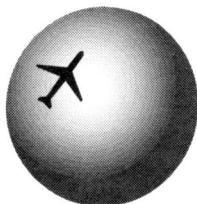

Figure 10.11 Marker design

Phase two: assigning artworks as marker design

① With the Selection tool active, select the artwork.

② Choose Design… from the Graphs sub-menu in the Object menu. The Graph Design dialog box will be displayed (see Figure 10.8).

③ Click New Design. The design will be listed and shown in the Preview window.

④ Click Rename and enter a name in the Name field.

⑤ Click OK to return to the Graph Design dialog box. Then click OK again.

Phase three: incorporating marker designs in graphs

① With the Group-selection tool active, double or treble-click one of the existing markers to select all related markers.

② Choose Marker... from the Graphs sub-menu in the Object menu. The Marker dialog box will be displayed.

③ Under Choose Marker Design, select one of the named designs. The marker will be scaled to the size of the default squares (see Figure 10.12).

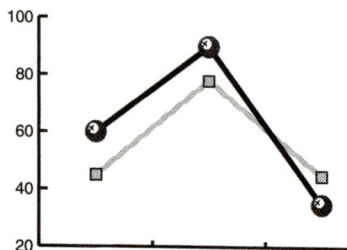

Figure 10.12 Graph with a custom marker design, in this case enlarged

▲ See Graph workthroughs later in this chapter on how to enlarge markers within a graph.

Setting graph options

Options available to all graph types

Axis position

The value axis can be on the left or right side, or both (except pie charts, which are axis-free).

Axis tick marks and labels

Tick marks, indicating the units of measurements, can be set horizontally or vertically, or both.

Drop shadows

Drop shadows can be added to all graphs, but are less appropriate for line and scatter graphs.

Legend position

Legends can be displayed vertically to the right of a graph or horizontally at the top of a graph.

Overlapping columns and areas

Columns and areas can be overlapped or not and the order of overlap specified.

Options specific to graph types

Column and stacked column

The space between columns and clusters of columns can be altered.

Bar and stacked bar

The space between bars and clusters of columns can be altered.

Line

Data points can be marked and connected, and if connected the draw lines can be filled. Also lines can be added from edge to edge.

Area

No options are available.

Scatter

Same as line graphs, except edge-to-edge lines can't be specified.

Pie

You can choose to have no legends, legends within the wedge shapes or standard legends. Wedges can be sorted in the order you entered the data (None), from largest to smallest value (All) or in the order of the graph containing the largest value (First). Multiple pie graphs can be scaled proportionately (Ratio), scaled the same (Even) or stacked and scaled in proportion (Stacked).

Radar

Same as line graphs, except edge-to-edge lines can't be specified.

Combining graph types in a graph

① With the Selection tool active, select the whole graph.

② Select Type… from the Graphs sub-menu in the Object menu. The Graph Type dialog box will be displayed.

③ Choose Both sides from the Value Axis pop-up menu.

④ Click OK.

⑤ Deselect the graph.

⑥ With the Group-selection tool active, double or treble-click the legend and related column(s) you wish to change to another type.

⑦ Select Type… from the Graphs sub-menu in the Object menu. The Graph Type dialog box will be displayed.

⑧ Under Type, select a different graph type, except Scatter.

⑨ Click OK.

Graph workthroughs

Creating graphs with longer or shorter columns

There are two ways to alter the proportion of graphs to give longer or shorter columns.

One way is to experiment with different dimensions when you first create a graph. Through trial and error you will finally arrive at the proportions you require.

Alternatively, you can distort a completed graph by scaling it. You will distort type along with the graph objects so you will need to correct any size and horizontal/vertical scale changes.

Creating graphs with larger markers

Illustrator tends to create markers which are too small to convey design detail. The only way to increase their size is to scale them locally after the markers are in place. Just select each marker in turn and enlarge them using the Scale command.

Editing graphs

Objects within graphs can be manipulated as any other Illustrator objects. Using the Direct-select tool, you can move paths around, assign different fills and strokes and alter font attributes. Provided you do not ungroup a graph, it will retain its graphing properties. By this I mean that it will allow you to amend its data and type dialog boxes in the normal manner. Ungroup a chart, and such controls become inaccessible.

Summary

Graph attributes Graph attributes defined within the graphing dialog boxes can be modified at will, provided graph objects remain grouped.

Graph data Graph labels and data need to suit graph types for meaningful results to emerge.

Column/marker designs You can create your own column and marker artworks for integration into standard graphs to meet specific design needs.

Graph options Options for axis position, tick marks, labels, drop shadows and legend position are available for most graph types.

Combination graphs Graph types can be combined within a graph to aid communication.

Workthroughs Two useful workthroughs allow you to get around the limitations of Illustrator's graph controls.

11 | WORKING WITH TYPE

Adding type

Type can be added in a number of ways within Illustrator.

You can create lines of type directly on the artboard or as columns within type containers. Either way you create type using the Type tool.

You can also create type that follows a path – curved type is achieved by this means – and you can fill objects with type to create shaped areas. These type configurations are created using the Path Type and Area Type tools. Variants of these tools allow you to set type vertically – characters stacked on top of each other instead of lining up in a row.

Furthermore, you can apply non-type attributes to type by converting it to outlines. However, once converted, they become ordinary Illustrator objects and can't be edited using the type controls.

Whatever its configuration, type is edited in the same way.

Creating lines of type

Short pieces of text, such as headings and captions, are achieved by typing directly on the artboard. The baselines of type set in this manner attach to non-printing horizontal paths. Such type doesn't self-wrap so the use of returns or shift-returns is essential for multi-lined texts.

Lines of type created this way are often aligned with ruler guides or grids for accurate positioning.

> ① With the Type tool active, click on artboard at the point where you wish the top left of your type to be.
>
> ② Type in text using the keyboard (see Figure 11.1).

Lino

Figure 11.1 A single line of type

Creating a column of type

Columns of type are achieved through the use of type containers. The lines of type bounded by such containers automatically wrap when they reach their edges.

Like lines of type, type containers are often aligned with ruler guides or grids.

① With the Type tool active, click-drag diagonally on artboard to define the column area. A type container will be created.

② Type in text using the keyboard (see Figure 11.2).

  If you are unable to see any or all of the text enlarge the type container.

Columns, three-quarter and
half columns; pilasters; the
conjunction of columns with
arches, intercolumniation,

Figure 11.2 A single column of type within a type container

▲ Use the Vertical Type tool to create vertical lines of stacked characters.

Resizing type containers

① With any Selection tool active, click once somewhere within the container (if it is not already selected) and move the pointer to one of its handles. Don't press the mouse button when you do this.

② The pointer turns into a double-arrow. Click-drag the handle to resize the column (see Figure 11.3).

▲ Handles halfway along the side of type containers can be used to enlarge or reduce their width or height. Corner handles enable you to alter both dimensions at once.

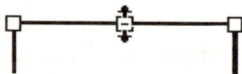

Figure 11.3 Resizing a type container

Entering text, returns and spaces

Sometimes you will find it easier to enter text accurately with the hidden characters showing, i.e. the symbols which represent non-printing characters, such as spaces or returns (see Figure 11.4).

Text will automatically run into the next line when it reaches the right edge of a type container so there is no need to use returns at the end of each line.

However, you need to use returns for lines of type without a container.

Type in upper and lower case unless you're sure the text will remain in capitals. Unlike in other programs, the only way to alter the case of type is to enter it in afresh.

Showing hidden characters

● Choose Show Hidden Characters from the Type menu.

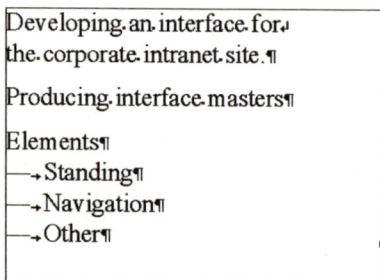

Figure 11.4 Text showing hidden characters

Starting a new paragraph

● Press Return

Starting a new line

Use these keystrokes to control line breaks within such text as a heading, address or verse:

● Press [Shift] + [Return]

Entering a normal word space

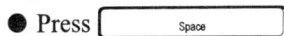

● Press [Space]

Importing text from a word-processing file

Text can be imported from most word-processing (and ASCII) files. Illustrator imports all the text in a file, complete with page breaks, etc. You might wish to bring in only part of a document. If so, copy and paste the text using the clipboard or split the word-processed document into a number of smaller documents first and then import text from each file in turn.

Importing text

① Choose Place... from the File menu. A directory dialog box will be displayed.

② Use the directory dialog box controls to locate the text file.

③ Click OK. The loaded cursor indicates that text is ready to be placed.

Either: click on artboard at the point you wish the top left of your text to be.

Or: click-drag diagonally on artboard to define a column area.

▲ When importing text to be placed in different parts of your artwork, import the text into a temporary type container positioned in a blank area or to one side of the artboard. Then cut and paste the text from this container elsewhere. Delete this temporary container after use.

Seeing all text in a column

If text is overfilling a container, a small plus sign square will be displayed (see Figure 11.5). The presence of this sign indicates that not all text is visible. It's good practice to make adjustments to remove the sign even if the only hidden text comprises paragraph returns.

Showing all text in a column

● Deepen or widen the container.

Or: link it to another container.

Or: shorten the text (see Basic text editing below).

Or: alter the type attributes. See Basic formatting (page 152).

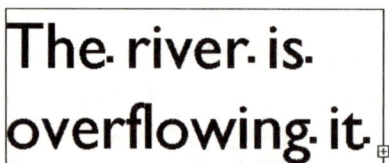

The· river· is· overflowing· it·

Figure 11.5 The presence of the plus sign in a small square at the bottom right of a container indicates that there is more text to be displayed

Basic text editing

You edit text within Illustrator in much the same way as you do in most word-processing programs. You select the text and then add or delete text using the keyboard and copy or move text using the clipboard.

Selecting text

Text needs to be selected for editing and formatting purposes. Text is selected by using either one of the Type tools, which are the primary editing tools, or one of the selection tools (see Figure 11.6). When one of the Type tools is active, the dotted rectangle framing the I-beam cursor automatically disappears when positioned over text.

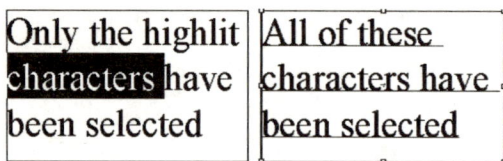

Only the highlit characters have been selected

All of these characters have been selected

Figure 11.6 Characters selected using the type tool (left) and using the Selection tool (right)

Use the type tools when you wish to select parts of text, whether it's set on a line or within a container, and the selection tools when you wish to select all text. Only the selection tools allow you to select non-contiguous text – unconnected text at various locations within your artwork.

▲ When selecting text, try to click to a regular beat and keep the body of the mouse steady.

Selecting text using one of the type tools

Text to be selected	Number of clicks
● Any contiguous text	Click-drag over text
● Whole word (with space after)	Click twice on word
● Whole paragraph	Click three times within paragraph

Selected characters in text are highlighted in colour.

Selecting text using one of the selection tools

Text to be selected	Number of clicks
● Whole line or container	Click once on line or within container

Moving and copying text using the clipboard

Moving and copying text is normally done using the clipboard (a short-term storage area assigned for this purpose). Any text which you cut or copy is automatically placed on the clipboard.

However many times you paste, text will remain on the clipboard until another piece of text is cut or copied.

Moving text

① Select the text you wish to move, by using one of the methods described previously.

② Choose Cut from the Edit menu.

③ Position the insertion point where you wish to place the text (make sure it's 'blinking' within the line of text or container).

④ Select Paste from the Edit menu.

▲ If you select text instead of positioning the insertion point and choose Paste from the Edit menu, the pasted text will replace the selected text.

Copying text

① Select the text you wish to copy, by using one of the methods described previously.

② Choose Copy from the Edit menu.

③ Position the insertion point where you wish to place the copied text (make sure it's 'blinking' within the line of text or container).

④ Select Paste from the Edit menu.

▲ If you select text instead of positioning the insertion point and choose Paste from the Edit menu, the pasted text will replace the selected text.

Deleting text

Either:

● Select the text and press [Delete] (back space).

Or:

● Position the insertion point to one side of the text to be deleted and press either [Delete] (back space) or [⌦].

Adding in extra text

① Position the insertion point where you wish to add text (make sure it's 'blinking' within the line of text or container).

② Type in the additional text.

Deleting whole lines of text and containers

① With the Selection tool active, click on line of text or within type container.

② Press [Delete].

Basic formatting

To meet your design needs, all the text you include within an artwork will need to be given basic formatting, including such attributes as font, size, leading and alignment.

The first two attributes can be applied within the Type menu or by using the Character palette. Leading can be applied only within the Character palette and alignment within the Paragraph palette.

Applying essential attributes

① Select the text to be styled using one of the methods described under Selecting text (page 150).

② Choose Character... from the Type menu palette. The Character palette will be displayed.

③ Choose Paragraph... from the Type menu palette. The Paragraph palette will be displayed.

④ Choose a font from either the Font sub-menu in the Type menu or the Font pop-up menu in the Character palette.

⑤ Choose a size from the Size sub-menu in the Type menu or from the Size pop-up menu in the Character palette.

⑥ Choose a value from the Leading pop-up menu in the Character palette. For normal text sizes (9–11 pt), the leading is usually 1–2 pt greater than the font size.

⑦ Click one of the alignment buttons in the Paragraph palette.

▲ Since the Character and Paragraph palettes are often used in sequence, nest them together to save time (see page 13).

▲ It makes sense to apply any common or dominant style attributes in one operation. Select *all* the text within a type container or on a set of lines and apply these attributes. Other attributes can then be applied to just parts of the text. You are less likely to leave any text unstyled working this way and it's far quicker.

✦ Auto leading is useful when initially sizing type, as it self adjusts to suit the font size. However, once you have chosen the font size, specify a value in points, unless the type is restricted to a single line.

Creating curved lines of type

Forcing text to follow a path

① Create an open or a closed path.

② With one of the Path-type tools selected, click anywhere on path segment.

③ Type in text using the keyboard. The text will follow the line of the path (see Figure 11.7).

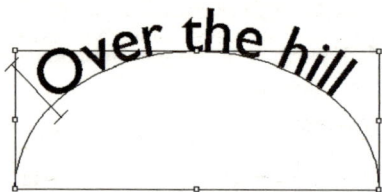

Figure 11.7 Selected object showing type following path. The I-beam can be seen before the capital O

Moving text along a path

① With the Selection tool active, select path.

② Position the pointer on the I-beam in the line of type.

③ Click-drag along, but not across, path.

Flipping the direction of text

① With the Selection tool active, position the pointer on the I-beam in the line of type.

② Double-click I-beam.

▲ Use Baseline Shift to move text across a path without changing its direction.

Creating shaped type areas

Forcing text to fill a closed path

① Create a closed path.

② With one of the Area-type tools selected, click on path (make sure you don't click within area of object).

③ Type in text using the keyboard. The text will begin to fill the internal area of the path (see Figure 11.8).

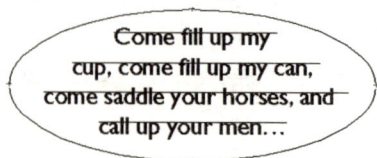

Figure 11.8 Selected object showing type within path

▲ An object containing text is automatically given no fill and no stroke. Use the Direct-selection tool to select its path in order to refill or restroke it.

Formatting paragraphs

Formatting can be applied at a character or paragraph level within Illustrator. Character attributes can apply to any contiguous text, whether it's all the text within a type container or just a single character, whilst paragraph attributes always apply to whole paragraphs or multiples of paragraphs.

As in most DTP and word-processing programs, paragraphs in Illustrator are defined by paragraph returns. These returns separate one paragraph from another and are entered using the Return key.

Alignment settings are paragraph attributes, as are indents, inter-paragraph spaces and tabs.

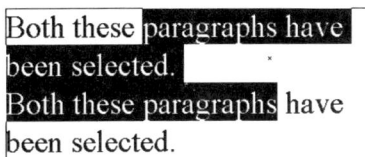

Both these paragraphs have been selected.
Both these paragraphs have been selected.

Figure 11.9 Paragraphs do not have to be fully selected for paragraph attributes to be applied

Indenting first lines of paragraphs

First-line indents are conventionally used to identify paragraph starts.

① Select a paragraph or paragraphs using one of the methods previously described.

② Choose Paragraph… from the Type menu. The Paragraph palette will be displayed (see Figure 11.10).

③ Enter a value in the First Line Left Indent field. You can do this either by clicking one of the small triangles or by typing.

④ Click OK to implement a setting you've typed in.

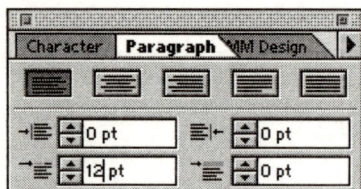

Figure 11.10 Setting a first line indent

Indenting both sides of paragraphs

Left and right indents may be used to reduce the width of paragraphs within type containers.

① Select a paragraph or paragraphs using one of the methods previously described.

② Choose Paragraph... from the Type menu. The Paragraph palette will be displayed.

③ Enter a value in the both the Left Indent and Right Indents fields. You can do this by either clicking the small triangles or by typing (see Figure 11.11).

④ Click OK to implement a setting you've typed in.

▲ When entering indents, where possible enter multiples or fractions of the font size in points: for example, if the text font size is 12 pt, choose say 12 pt, 6 pt or 18 pt.

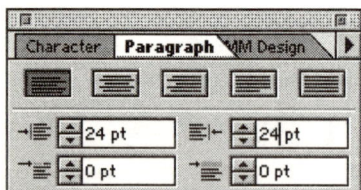

Figure 11.11 Indenting left and right edges of a paragraph

Hanging indents

Hanging indents are used for listing work, where numbers, letters or bullet points occupy a space to the left of the main bulk of the text to which they refer (see Figure 11.12).

① Select a paragraph or paragraphs using one of the methods previously described.

② Choose Paragraph… from the Type menu. The Paragraph palette will be displayed.

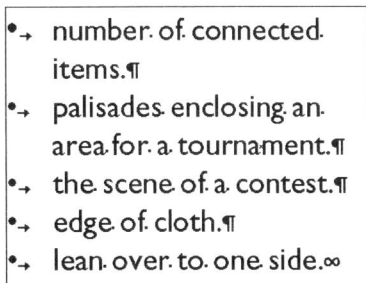

•→ number. of. connected.
   items.¶
•→ palisades. enclosing. an.
   area.for. a. tournament.¶
•→ the. scene. of. a. contest.¶
•→ edge. of. cloth.¶
•→ lean. over. to. one. side.∞

Figure 11.12 Paragraphs with hanging indents. A left aligned tab has been added to align the first words in each line

③ Enter a value in the Left Indent field (such as 20 pt) and a negative value in First Line Left Indent field (such as –20 pt). You can do this by clicking the small triangles or by typing (see Figure 11.13).

④ Click OK to implement these settings.

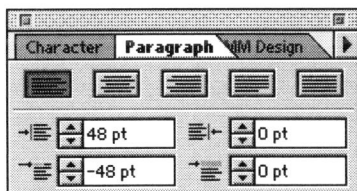

Figure 11.13 Setting a hanging indent using positive and negative values

▲ If you wish the first words after a tab character to align, a left-aligned tab needs to be inserted (see page 165).

Inserting spaces before paragraphs

Use inter-paragraph spacing to reduce typographic density and to create visual pauses between paragraphs. You can also use spaces between paragraphs as an alternative to first line indents.

Inserting paragraph spaces

① First remove any empty paragraphs (i.e. double ¶ symbols) from your text, by positioning the insertion point within each empty paragraph and pressing [Delete] (back space).

② Select a paragraph or paragraphs using one of the methods previously described.

③ Choose Paragraph… from the Type menu. The Paragraph palette will be displayed.

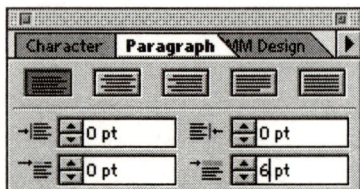

Figure 11.14 Inserting a space before a paragraph

④ Enter a value in the Space Before field. You can do this by clicking the small triangles or by typing (see Figure 11.14).

⑤ Click OK to implement a setting you've typed in.

▲ When entering spaces before and after paragraphs, where possible enter multiples or fractions of the text leading value in points: for example, if the leading is 15 pt, choose say 10 pt, 7.5 pt or 5 pt.

✦ Leading is introduced above lines and so a very large leading value applied to the first line of a paragraph will have the effect of visually increasing the space above it.

Spacing words

You can alter word and character spaces to improve the design, copyfitting, legibility or readability of text. The control within Illustrator is called tracking and is measured 1/1000th of an em space (an em space being roughly the width of a capital M). Untracked word and character spaces are set at 0 (see Figure 11.15).

① Select the text to be tracked using one of the methods previously described.

② Choose Character… from the Type menu. The Character palette will be displayed.

s p a c e d   o u t

o u t e r   s p a c e

Figure 11.15 Both lines have been 'tracked' for visual effect

③ Enter a value in the Tracking field. You can do this by clicking the small triangles or by typing (see Figure 11.16).

A positive figure, such as 100, will widen the spacing; a negative figure, such as –50, will tighten the spacing.

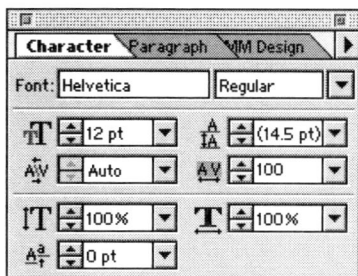

Figure 11.16 Tracking characters by 100/1000 em

▲ When tracking text for copyfitting reasons, apply tracking to complete lines or, even better, complete paragraphs and use the minimum setting possible. Then tracking won't be too obvious to the reader.

Improving the spacing between characters

You can correct poor intercharacter spacing and create interesting character juxtapositions by kerning (see Figure 11.17). Like tracking, kerning is measured in one 1/1000th of an em space with unkerned spaces set at 0.

Adjusting inter-character spaces

① Position the insertion point between two characters within a word. The text should not be highlighted in any way.

② Choose Character... from the Type menu. The Character palette will be displayed.

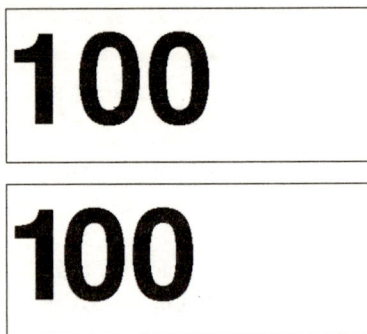

Figure 11.17 The figures 1 and 0 are too wide apart (top). The figures are kerned to decrease the spacing between them

③ Enter a value in the Kerning field. You can do this by clicking the small triangles or by typing (see Figure 11.18).

A positive figure, such as 100, will widen the inter-character spacing; a negative figure such as –50 will tighten the inter-character spacing.

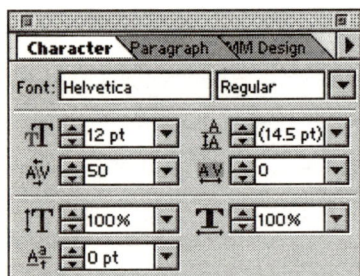

Figure 11.18 Kerning characters by 50/1000 em

Adjusting the baseline position of text

Text can be moved up or down relative to its normal baseline position (see Figure 11.19). The control which governs its position is called baseline shift. Baseline shift is similar to the superscript/subscript typestyle but is user definable. It can be used to 'cheat' the leading – to move parts of lines up or down, when the required effect can't be achieved through leading adjustment. It also provides a means of moving a line of type up or down within a shallow type container.

① Select the text to be shifted using one of the methods described under Selecting text, page 150.

② Choose Character… from the Type menu. The Character palette will be displayed (see Figure 11.8).

Choose Show Options in the pop-up menu if the Baseline Shift field is not showing.

③ Enter a value in the baseline Shift field. You can do this by clicking the small triangles or by typing.

④ Click OK to implement a setting you've typed in.

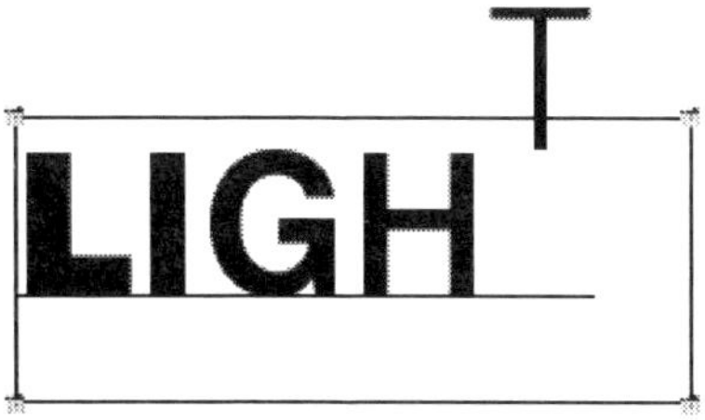

Figure 11.19 A character is shifted from its normal baseline position

Incremental type adjustment

The following keystroke short-cuts are useful for sizing, leading, tracking and shifting the baselines of type.

Altering font sizes incrementally

● Increase by 2 pt increments: ⌘ Shift + >

● Decrease by 2 pt increments: ⌘ Shift + <

In Windows use the Control key instead of the Command key.

▲ Hold down Alt in addition to the above for 10 pt increments.

Altering leading incrementally

● Increase by 1pt increments: Option + ↑

● Decrease by 1pt increments: Option + ↓

▲ Hold down Command (Control) in addition to the above for 10 pt increments.

Altering kerning/tracking incrementally

- Increase by 0.020 em increments: [⌘] [Shift] + [}]
- Decrease by 0.020 em increments: [⌘] [Shift] + [{]

    In Windows use the Control key instead of the Command key.

Altering baseline shift incrementally

- Increase by 2 pt increments: [Alt] [Shift] + [↑]
- Decrease by 2 pt increments: [Alt] [Shift] + [↓]

▲ Hold down Command (Control) in addition to the above for 10 pt increments.

Linking columns

You can link any number of type containers together so that text flows between them. The containers can either be single column or multi-column, it makes no difference. This feature is particularly useful as it keeps text in one piece for ease of editing – obviating the need to cut and paste, which can easily lead to errors.

Linking two or more type containers

① With the Selection tool active, select the column to be linked.

② Choose Blocks Link from the Type menu.

Unlinking type containers

① With the Selection tool active, select the columns to be unlinked.

② Choose Blocks Unlink from the Type menu.

Creating a linked type container

① Choose Artwork from the View menu.

② With the Direct-selection tool active, position the pointer over the centre point of the container holding the text. (If the centre point is not showing select the text container and click the Show centre button in the Attributes palette.)

③ Hold down ⌥[Option] and click-drag from the centre point to create a linked copy of the container. The type flows from the first container into the new container provided there is enough overflow text to do this.

④ Choose Transform Again from the Transform sub-menu in the Object menu for each additional linked container.

▲ Use the Group-selection tool to move linked containers independently of one another.

Creating rows and columns within containers

Type containers can be divided up into rows and columns for tabular or general text work. As each division become a text container in its own right they can be given fill and strokes independently of one another (see Figure 11.20).

① Create a type container in the normal manner. Make sure it's large enough to be split up into rows and columns.

② With the Selection tool active, choose Rows and Columns... from the Type menu. The Rows and Columns dialog box will be displayed.

③ Under Rows, enter values in the Number and Gutter fields. The Height field will automatically be entered for you.

④ Under Columns, enter values in the Number and Gutter fields. The Width field will automatically be entered for you.

⑤ Under Options, click a Text flow button.

⑥ Check or tick Add Guides if you wish guides to be added to the artboard.

⑦ Click OK.

	Excursion	Versailles	Giverny
PanoVision	Adult	£21	£37
	Child 4–11	£10.50	£18.50
Disc Tours	Adult	£29	n/a
	Child 4–11	£15	n/a

Figure 11.20 A type container converted into twenty smaller containers presented as four columns and five rows. The two right hand columns are shown in Preview selection mode.

▲ You can force text to move from container to container by entering Returns. Before you do this it's best to format your text to create the optimum number of lines within each container.

You can alter the dimensions of individual containers and delete containers without affecting the text flow. You can also add linked containers as described in the previous section. Text flows into any new linked container and then back into the next container in the row or column.

Wrapping text around an object

You can wrap text around objects and images framed by objects (see Figure 11.21). You can also wrap text around the edge of cutout images, provided they have clipping paths.

① Position an object over a column of text.

② With the Selection tool active, select both type container and object.

③ Choose Make from the Wrap sub-menu of the type menu.

Original colour wood engraving, 1983, numbered from the edition of twenty on parchment, signed in pencil, printed by Editions Parabos, Madrid, 1984 and published

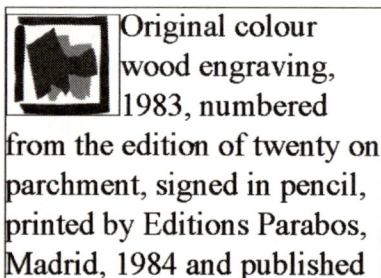

Fig. 11.21 Wrapping text around an object

Unwrapping text around an object

① With the Selection tool active, select either the column or object.

② Choose Release from the Wrap sub-menu of the type menu.

Tabulating text

Multi-column tables can be created by applying bespoke tab positions to individual paragraphs within tabbed text. These bespoke tabs override the default 0.5 inch tab positions which are left aligned (see Figure 11.22).

The Tab key is used to insert tabs within text. Tabs should be entered wherever you wish to separate text into columns.

These can be inserted either within a WP document before it is placed within Illustrator or within Illustrator itself.

The Tabs Ruler is used to create new tab positions to any one of four different styles of column alignment.

It's important to remember that tabbing is a paragraph attribute; therefore any paragraph can have its own tab positions and alignments. Because of this, always try to avoid merging tabbed paragraphs accidentally as your formatting may go awry.

▲ When preparing text for tabbing, reduce the number of paragraphs within a table to the minimum. Use Shift-Returns to separate lines and use Returns only to separate those lines between which you wish to insert paragraph spaces, rules or different tabbing. Always avoid having tabs at end of lines with text wrapping from line to line.

Accessing the Tab Ruler

① Select a paragraph or paragraphs within the table using one of the methods previously described.

② Choose Tab Ruler... from the Type menu. The Tab Ruler will be displayed (see Figure 11.22).

▲ If you move the Tab Ruler and wish to return it to its original position, click the small box at the right-hand top corner of the palette.

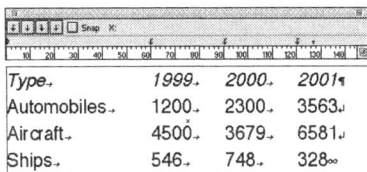

Figure 11.22 Tab rule aligned to type container with hidden characters showing

Setting new tab positions

① Click above tab ruler to position a new tab.

② Click a Tab Style button.

③ The text in the text box will automatically move to the new tab position if a tab character has previously been entered. If the tab is incorrectly positioned, click-drag the tab icon to a new position on the ruler.

④ Repeat stages 1–3 until all the tabs have been inserted and correctly positioned.

⑤ Click OK.

▲ To snap tabs to ruler increments, check or tick Snap.

✚ As new tabs are applied, all the unseen default tabs to the left of the new tabs(s) are automatically removed.

Removing tabs from the Tabs Ruler

① Either: click-drag a tab off the top or left side of ruler.

② Replace tabs, if required, and click OK.

Converting type to outlines

Type can be converted to ordinary objects within Illustrator (see Figure 11.23). The benefits of conversion are twofold:

- non-type attributes can be applied to letterforms
- documents aren't reliant on external fonts.

Converted letterforms can be manipulated as normal Illustrator objects – which they have become – to create logos and other typographic devices.

Complex typographic work can be developed employing many fonts with the knowledge that once the fonts are converted, artworks can be output without fuss.

Remember, once type is converted, it is not possible to further edit or alter its letterforms using Illustrator's type controls.

▲ Lettershapes with counters (internal shapes) are invariably compounded to give transparency (see page 114).

Converting type to outlines

① Create some type in the normal way.

② With the Selection tool active, select the type.

③ Choose Create Outlines from the Type menu.

④ Edit paths in the normal manner.

❗ This technique works only when Truetype fonts are used or when Adobe Type 1 fonts are used with Adobe Type Manager (ATM) in operation.

Figure 11.23 Type (left) converted to outlines (middle) and edited (right). All steps shown in artwork mode

Summary

Adding text Text can be entered as lines of type either directly on the artboard or within type containers.

Linked columns Type containers can be linked so text can flow from column to column.

Invisible characters It's easier to enter text accurately with the characters representing returns, tabs and suchlike showing.

Formatting Type is formatted at a character or paragraph level.

Curved and shaped text Type can be made to follow a path or to fill the shape of an object.

Columns and rows Text containers can be divided into columns and rows for tabular work.

Modifying typeforms Type can be converted to paths and edited as Illustrator objects.

12 | IMPORTING AND EXPORTING ARTWORK

Importing images

Images can be included within artwork in a number of ways. Depending on the image type images can be:

- dragged and dropped from other documents
- cut/copied and pasted using the clipboard
- opened as an Illustrator document
- placed as linked images.

Dragging and dropping

You can drag and drop artwork between Illustrator documents and between Illustrator documents and the desktop. When dropping on the desktop, the artworks are copied as a PICT clipping file (on the Macintosh) or a Scrap Metafile (in Windows).

You can also drag and drop between Illustrator and Photoshop 4 (or later) documents. Illustrator objects are automatically converted to bitmap images when copied across into Photoshop. Photoshop images are automatically converted to 72 ppi resolution and to RGB colour mode when copied across to Illustrator. Holding down ⌘ enables Illustrator paths to be copied across into Photoshop.

Dragging and dropping into Photoshop

① Select the artwork you wish to copy.

② Open the Photoshop document into which you wish to copy the selection.

③ Drag the selection into the Photoshop document window. A black outline will appear.

④ Release the mouse button.

Using the clipboard

You can copy images from other documents and move or copy images within Illustrator using the clipboard.

However many times you paste, an image will remain on the clipboard until other content is cut or copied, which takes its place on the clipboard.

Moving images

① With the Selection tool active, select the image you wish to move. Choose Cut from the Edit menu.

② Choose Paste from the Edit menu in order to paste the image in the new location.

Copying images

① With the Selection tool active, select the image you wish to copy. Choose Copy from the Edit menu in order to paste the copy of the image in the desired location.

② Choose Paste from the Edit menu.

Opening as an illustrator document

① Choose Open… from the Illustrator's File menu. The Open directory dialog box will be displayed.

② Use the directory dialog box controls to locate your document.

③ Click Open. The document window will be displayed.

Placing linked images

When you select the Link option when placing and pasting images into an Illustrator document, low-resolution bitmap versions of these images are copied into your document for layout purposes. Links between the low-res images and their hi-res counterparts are automatically made during the placement process.

When you output your documents, Illustrator takes the data detailing the position and scaling of the low-res images and applies it to the hi-res images which it uses for outputting purposes.

Placing images

① Choose Place … from the File menu. A directory dialog box will be displayed (see Figure 12.1).

② Use the directory dialog box controls to locate the image.

③ Check or tick Link.

④ Click Open.

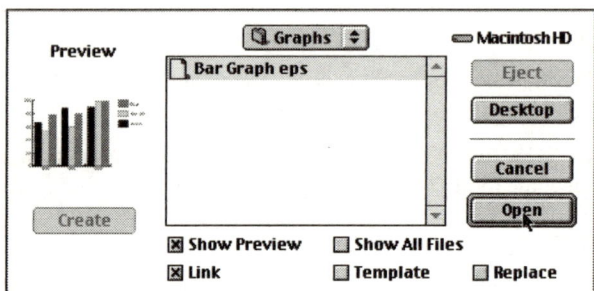

Figure 12.1 The Place directory dialog box

▲ If you wish to edit EPS files within Illustrator, uncheck or untick Link before placing.

Images are selected, moved, transformed and deleted as Illustrator objects. They can also be cropped by masking.

! Avoid enlarging images more than 165%, as image degradation may take place when outputting.

Managing linked files

If you alter and resave a linked image using the application that created it, when you next use the Illustrator file containing the image, it will automatically be updated.

Editing a linked image

① Close the Illustrator file containing the linked image you wish to alter.

② Open the linked file using its creator application, such as Photoshop.

③ Make any necessary alterations.

④ Save the file at the same location and under the same name.

⑤ Reopen the Illustrator file containing the linked image. The artwork will automatically be updated

Getting info on a linked file

① Select the placed image.

② Choose Selection Info... from the File menu. The Selection Info dialog box will be displayed (see Figure 12.2).

③ Choose Linked images from the Info pop-up menu.

④ View the listed information.

⑤ Click Done.

```
┌─────────────────────────────────────────────────┐
│                 Selection Info                   │
│  Info: [ Linked Images        ⬦ ]    ┌─────────┐ │
│                                      │  Done   │ │
│  ┌────────────────────────────────┐  └─────────┘ │
│  │ Linked Images:              ▲  │  ┌─────────┐ │
│  │                                │  │  Save   │ │
│  │ Macintosh HD:Images:Buchanan tiff │ └─────────┘ │
│  │ Type: Grayscale                │             │
│  │ Bits per Pixel: 8              │             │
│  │ Channels: 1                    │             │
│  │ Size: 4698K, 1952 by 2465 pixels │           │
│  │ Dimensions: 468.48 by 591.6 points │         │
│  │ Resolution: 300 by 300 pixels per inch │     │
│  │                             ▼  │             │
│  └────────────────────────────────┘             │
└─────────────────────────────────────────────────┘
```

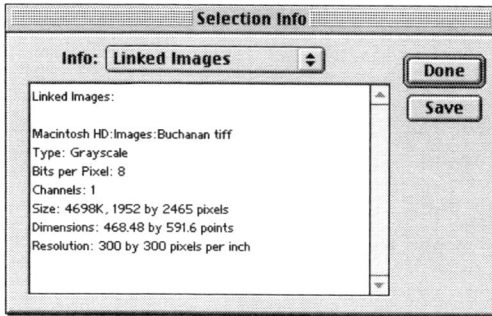

Figure 12.2 The Selection Info dialog box

▲ If you wish all linked files to be listed do not select any images before accessing this dialog box.

Assigning URL links

You can assign a URL string to any object within Illustrator. When you export the artwork in either GIF89a or JPEG file format the resultant file becomes an imagemap.

Linking an object to a URL

① Select the object.

② Choose Show Attributes from the Window menu. The Attributes palette will be displayed.

③ Enter a URL into the URL field. The URL must begin with http://.

④ If you have a Web browser on your system, you can verify the URL by clicking Launch browser.

! When you export your artwork as a GIF89a or JPEG select the Imagemap option and click Client-side. By selecting Client-side two files are saved, the .jpg or .gif file and an HTML file containing the link information. These two files must be saved in the same location for the Web application to interpret the imagemap

Rasterizing artwork

Illustrator objects can be rasterized – converted to bitmap images – within an artwork. The main advantage of doing this is that Photoshop-style filters can be applied (see next section).

① With the Selection tool active, select object(s).

② Choose Rasterize from the Object menu. The Rasterize dialog box will be displayed (see Figure 12.3).

③ Choose an option in the Colour Model pop-up menu.

④ Select or enter a resolution.

⑤ Check or tick Anti-Alias in most cases.

⑥ Click OK.

▲ See the section Rasterizing artwork later in this chapter for a discussion on aliasing and resolutions.

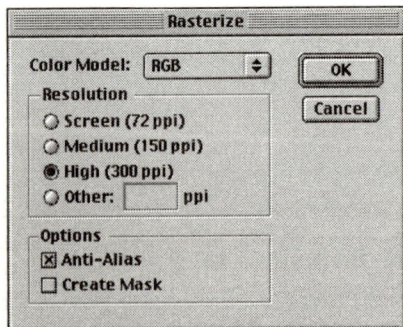

Rasterize

Color Model: [RGB ◆]   [OK]

Resolution
○ Screen (72 ppi)   [Cancel]
○ Medium (150 ppi)
● High (300 ppi)
○ Other: [   ] ppi

Options
☒ Anti-Alias
☐ Create Mask

Figure 12.3 The Rasterize dialog box

Applying filters to bitmap images

Some of the filters in Illustrator allow you to apply special effects to bitmap images embedded within your artwork. If an image is linked a copy is automatically made from the linked file. The filter is then applied to the embedded copy, leaving the original linked image intact.

The standard filters include: Artistic filters, Blur filters, Brush Stroke filters, Distort filters, Texture filters, Pixelate filters, Sketch filters and Video filters.

Using filters

Previewing and applying filters

① With the Selection tool active, select a bitmap image.

② Choose a filter from the sub-menus in the Filter menu.

③ If a dialog box is displayed, enter values and select options.

④ The effect is previewed within a preview window (in the case of filters involving dialog boxes).

⑤ Click-drag within this window to scroll around the image and click on the + or − buttons to zoom in or out.

⑥ Click OK to apply the filter.

Filter shortcuts

● Press ⌘ + . (period) to cancel a filter.

● Press ⌘ + Z to undo a filter.

● Press ⌘ + E to reapply.

● Press ⌘ Option + E to display the dialog box of the most recently used filter.

Exporting artwork

You can export artwork as bitmap images in a number of formats including BMP, GIF89a, JPEG, PCX, Photoshop 5, PICT (Mac only), PNG and TIFF.

Some formats allow you to choose from a number of resolutions and to decided whether artwork is to be anti-aliased or not (see Figure 12.4).

Anti-aliasing softens the staircasing effect you get with line work in bitmap images. However, it can make very small type illegible so occasionally you may wish to turn this setting off.

Only JPEG and GIF89a support artworks containing objects linked to a Uniform Resource Locator (URL) strings. Bitmap images incorporating such attributes are termed imagemaps.

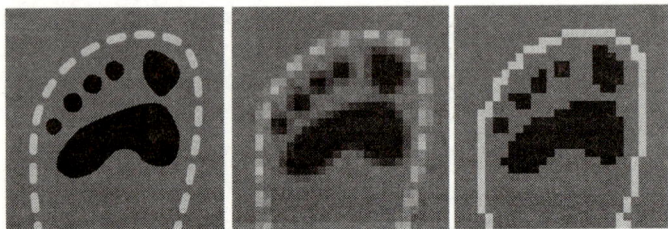

Figure 12.4 Illustrator artwork (left), aliased (centre) and anti-aliased (right)

① Choose Export… from the File menu. A directory dialog box will be displayed.

② Choose an option in the Format sub-menu.

③ Click Save. An appropriate dialog box will be displayed.

④ Select options as required.

⑤ Click OK.

▲ As the dimensions of exported artwork is defined by the overall dimensions of your artwork, any extraneous objects, such as released guides and stray points, should be deleted prior to exporting.

File formats explained

Illustrator will accept and export a multitude of file formats, including BMP, EPS, GIF89a, JPEG, PCX, PDF, PICT, PNG and TIFF (see Figure 12.5).

BMP

Bitmap images are often saved in BMP (Windows Bitmap). This is Windows' native Paint format. It can be used to save bilevel, grayscale and RGB images in 24-bit (see Figure 12.7).

File format	Save to	Place	Link	Export to
BMP	✗	✓	✓	✓
CorelDraw	✗	✓		✗
EPS	✓	✓	✓	✗
FreeHand 5.5+	✗	✓	–	✗
Illustrator	✓	✗	–	✗
JPEG	✗	✓	–	✓
PCX	✗	✓	–	✓
Photoshop 5	✗	✗	✓	✓
PICT File (Mac only)	✗	✓	✓	✓
PDF	✗	✓	✓	✗
PNG	✗	✓	–	✓
TIFF	✗	✓	✓	✓

Figure 12.5 Some file formats supported by Illustrator

EPS

Vectored drawn images are usually saved in Encapsulated PostScript (EPS), as are Bitmap images containing PostScript elements. This format was originally developed by Altsys – it is generic and comes in many forms. Drawings produced in Macromedia FreeHand and Illustrator, for instance, are saved in this format. It can be used to save bilevel, grayscale, RGB and CMYK colour images in 24-bit.

Like TIFF files, EPS files do not embed themselves within your document so you need to keep the original files for outputting purposes. As they are substantially larger than TIFFs – about a third again in size – it's best to avoid this format for bitmap images unless you really need its features.

GIF89a

Bitmap images are often saved in GIF89a (Graphics Interchange Format). This popular web format converts images to indexed-colour. The format supports interlacing, transparency and URL links (see Figure 12.6).

Generally speaking, the best colour rendition achievable within this format is gained by using the Adaptive palette (which weights the colours in the palette based on how frequently they are used in the original artwork).

However, images on the same web page may have their colours remapped on monitors with only 8-bit colour support.

This is avoided if you use the Web palette. Whilst it's restricted to 216 colours it has the advantage of being consistent in all situations.

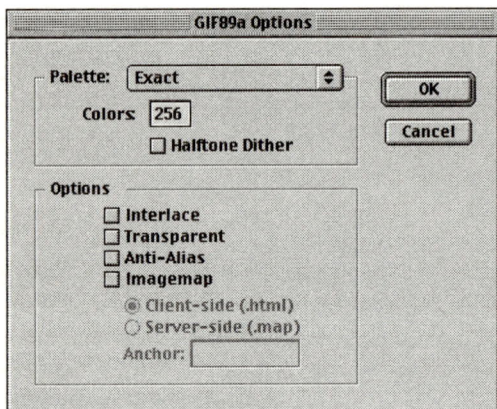

Figure 12.6 Exporting in GIF89a format

JPEG

Bitmap images are often saved in JPEG (Joint Photographic Experts Group) format. This format was developed for the newspaper publishing industry and has become a worldwide standard for transmitting images by modem. It can be used to save bilevel, grayscale, RGB and CMYK colour images in 24-bit with or without URL links.

Because this file format decimates data (it features a 'lossy' compression algorithm to reduce file sizes) it's not recommended for print production work.

PCX

Bitmap images are sometimes saved in PCX (Windows Bitmap) (see Figure 12.6). This is an old DOS PC Paintbrush format which is available in a number of versions. It can be used to save bilevel, grayscale and RGB in 24-bit (see Figure 12.7).

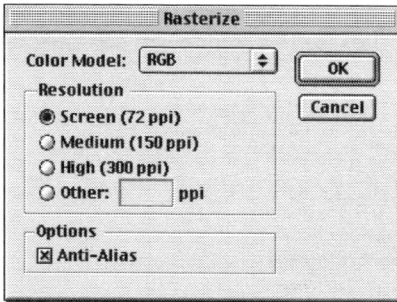

Figure 12.7 Exporting in BMP or PCX format

PICT

Vectored drawings/charts and bitmaps are often saved in PICT. This is Apple's native format and uses the same routines as the software that draws the Macintosh screen. It can be used to save bilevel, grayscale and RGB colour images up to 24-bit.

PICT files always embed themselves in their entirety within the document so you don't need to keep the original files for output. However, Illustrator file sizes will increase substantially if many images are imported in this format.

PDF

Whole documents are occasionally saved in Acrobat PDF (Portable Document Format). This format was developed by Adobe to meet the need for a single compact, device- and media-independent file which could be viewed and output on different and often remote devices without requiring originating programs, special print drivers or printer description files. PostScript pages, fonts, colours and vector and bitmap images are faithfully saved.

The format is increasingly used for storing pages on CD-ROMs, and for proofing documents onscreen.

PNG

Bitmap images can be saved in PNG format. Unlike GIF89a this new web format preserves all colour information in an image. The format supports

interlacing (the Adam7 option should be selected for this purpose) and
transparency and features the loss-less LZW compression algorithm to
reduce file sizes.

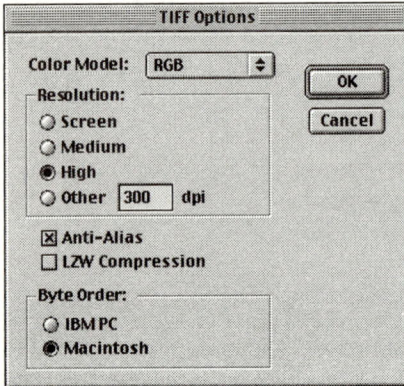

Figure 12.8 Exporting in TIFF format

TIFF

Bitmap images are usually saved in TIFF (Tagged Image File Format).
This format was originally developed by Microsoft and Aldus and has
become a standard worldwide. It can be used to save bilevel, grayscale,
RGB images up to 48-bit and CMYK images in 24-bit (see Figure 12.8).

TIFF files do not embed themselves within a document – they're tagged –
so you need to keep the original files for outputting purposes.

Choosing between GIF89a, JPEG and PNG

When exporting images for web pages, it's important that the most appropriate format is chosen (see Figure 12.9).

GIF89a works well for artworks containing horizontal runs of flat colour
as is the case in most Illustrator documents. However, it works less well
with artworks containing lots of pixel variation, such as those incorporating blends and/or bitmap images, as the maximum number of colours it
can support is 256.

In contrast, JPEG is good at dealing with pixel variation as it supports 24-bit colour but is poor at handling flat areas which tend to mosaic as a consequence of its compression method.

PNG is not only good at dealing with pixel variation (it supports 16-bit grayscale and 32-bit colour), it's also good at handling flat areas. And unlike GIF89a it supports variable transparency thus eliminating white haloes around images.

	GIF89a	JPEG	PNG
Compressing flat colours	good	poor	good
Compressing photographs	poor	good	good
Decompression speed	fast	slow	very fast
Ability to interlace	✓	✓	✓
Ability to support URLs	✓	✓	✗
Ability to have transparency	✓	✓	✓
Support for truecolour	✗	✓	✓

Figure 12.9 Web file formats compared

Specifying resolutions

For print

The resolution of bitmap images intended for printing should be roughly twice the halftone screen ruling of your final printing device, i.e. if your final printing device is a digital printer and its halftone screen is set at 60 lpi then the resolution of your image should be 120 ppi (dpi) or thereabouts. This calculation applies to both images imported into Illustrator artworks and artworks exported as bitmaps. You can, however, get reasonable results by multiplying the halftone screen ruling by one and a half or even by one, although both these settings give little flexibility for enlargement of images within Illustrator.

Most offset-litho work will be screened at between 100 and 200 lpi, the exact pitch depending on the surface smoothness of the paper to be printed on. Silkscreen work will usually be screened at no more than

100 lpi. Your printing company will be able to advise you on the halftone screen ruling for specific jobs.

If you are outputting using a stochastic or other type of dithered screen, set the image resolution to 150–300 ppi (dpi).

If your printing device prints in continuous tone set the image resolution to match the device's outputting resolution, which will probably be between 300 and 400 ppi (dpi).

▲ Always ask your printer for the screen size they propose to use for your job and inform the bureau of the size before they imageset your document.

For on-screen use

The resolution of images imported into artworks intended for on-screen delivery (such as for the Web) should be 72 ppi (dpi). The same resolution should be chosen when artworks are exported and saved in JPEG or GIF89a file formats .

Summary

Importing images Images can be imported by dragging and dropping, cutting and pasting, opening or placing.

Links Linked images are managed within the Links palette.

Rasterized objects Selected Illustrator objects can be converted to bitmap images within an artwork.

Special effects Bitmap images, whether rasterized internally or imported, can be given special effects.

Exported images Artworks can be exported as bitmap images for importation into Web or other on-screen documents.

File formats Many export formats are supported by Illustrator.

13 PREPARING FILES FOR PRINTING

Outputting from another computer

Illustrator documents can be directly printed using desktop printers or large digital colour presses (such as those made by Canon, Indigo and Xeikon). They can also be imageset at a bureau to produce bromide or film for subsequent photo litho printing.

Whichever method of output you employ, picture links need to be checked before final output and if you are outputting from a computer other than your own, you will also need to check the font usage.

Checking picture links

If you use the Link option when placing or pasting images within an Illustrator document, links are established between low-res images and their hi-res counterparts.

When you output your document, Illustrator uses the data in these files to reproduce the images. If it's unable to locate and use the original files, Illustrator will use instead the data in the embedded images for reproduction purposes. Reproduction by this means is inferior but will be adequate for copy proofing purposes.

If links between the images and their original files are inadvertently broken, they can easily be re-established using the Links palette. When an Illustrator document is opened, you will automatically be alerted if links are broken. Even so, it's best to check the status of all links on completion of a document, whether or not you think any links have been broken.

Checking picture linkage

① Choose Links from the Window menu. The Links palette will be displayed (see Figure 13.1).

② Look to the right of each listed image.

The presence of an Alert triangle will indicate an unlinked image. The lack of question mark indicates a linked image.

③ If an image is unlinked, click the Replace Link button. A directory dialog box will be displayed. Locate and select the missing file using the directory dialog box controls. Click Open.

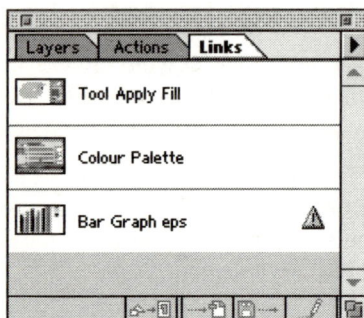

Figure 13.1 Alert triangle indicating a broken link

Font usage

Illustrator needs the correct fonts loaded when outputting documents and will ask for suitable substitute fonts if the specified fonts are not available. This almost invariably occurs when documents are output on other machines, such is the case when outputting at a bureau.

▲ Use the Macintosh or Windows system fonts if you wish to output without having to worry about font availability.

Checking font usage

① Choose Find Font… from the Type menu. The Find Font dialog box will be displayed (see Figure 13.2).

② View the fonts you've used in the Fonts in Document window.

③ Click Done to close the dialog box.

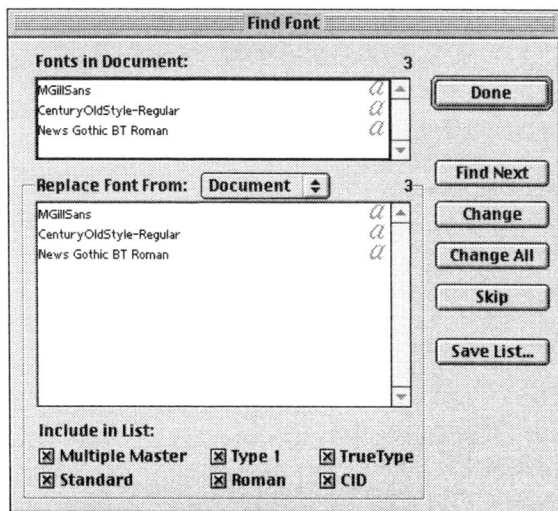

Figure 13.2 Checking the fonts used in a document

Proofing and printing artwork

Illustrator artworks can be output as grayscale or composite colour on either digital printers or proofers – the procedure is essentially the same for both types of device even though the purpose to which they are put differs.

Proofing as part of a quality-control process aims to simulate results on presses. You check proofs for colour fidelity, sharpness and other print attributes. Once approved, artwork is then output to imagesetters for conventional press work or to digital presses.

Printing, on the other hand, is an end in itself; artwork is output to digital printers or presses as the final product.

Outputting from page layout programs

Illustrator artworks imported into page layout documents can be proofed or printed along with other content using the host program controls. It is often far easier and faster to output this way and you don't need to learn further controls. All you need to do is save your Illustrator file in

Illustrator EPS format – first making sure that bitmap images and colours used in the artwork are correctly specified. Refer to relevant sections elsewhere in this book for information on these two areas.

Outputting artwork from Illustrator

If you are using Illustrator as your main program you will be outputting directly from Illustrator itself. You may also use its controls for proofing artworks you plan to later place elsewhere.

When proofing artworks, you will need to set crop marks to define where the printed sheets will eventually be trimmed (in the case of artworks containing multiple items, such as business cards, such marks are termed trim marks in Illustrator). You will also need one or other of these types of marks if outputting to a digital press.

Setting crop marks

You can create crop marks directly on your artwork using the Make crop-marks command.

    ① Using the Rectangle tool, create a rectangle to define the boundaries of the crop area.

    ② With the rectangle selected, choose Make from the Crop marks sub-menu in the Objects menu.

    ▲ If you wish the crop marks to match the size of your artboard and Single full page is selected in the Document Setup dialog box, there is no need to create a rectangle first.

Removing crop marks

    ● Choose Release from the Crop marks sub-menu in the Objects menu.

Only one set of crop marks can appear in a document. If you wish to include multiple marks, set trim marks instead (see Figure 13.3).

Setting trim marks

Trim marks define where different items within your artwork will be trimmed.

    ① Using the Rectangle tool, create a rectangle to define the boundaries of a crop area.

② With the rectangle selected, choose Trim from the Create sub-menu in the Filter menu.

③ Repeats steps 1 and 2 for each additional set of trim marks.

Figure 13.3 Business cards with trim marks in place

Removing trim marks

① With the Selection tool active, click the path.

② Press [Delete].

Specifying the page setup

① Choose Document Setup from the File menu. The Document Setup dialog box will be displayed.

On the Macintosh:

② Click Page Setup and then click Options. Your printer's set of controls will be displayed (see Figure 13.4). Alter the settings as required, click OK, then click OK to return to the Document Setup dialog box.

In Windows:

② Choose Printer Setup. Your printer's set of controls will be displayed. Alter the settings as required.

③ Click OK.

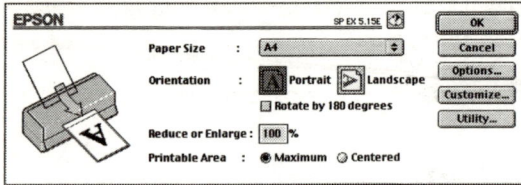

Figure 13.4 Typical Page Setup controls (Epson Stylus Photo EX)

Outputting a document

① Choose Print… from the File menu. The set of print controls will be displayed (see Figure 13.5).

② Enter the number of copies of each page required in the Copies field.

③ Under Pages, click All or either a sequence of pages, such as 1–1, or 3–4.

The number of pages that can be printed is determined by the View options selected in the Document Setup dialog box. If Single Page is selected, only single page will print. If either of the other view options is selected, you can specify a page or a range of pages to be printed.

④ Choose Composite from the Output pop-up menu, unless greyed.

⑤ Click Print or OK.

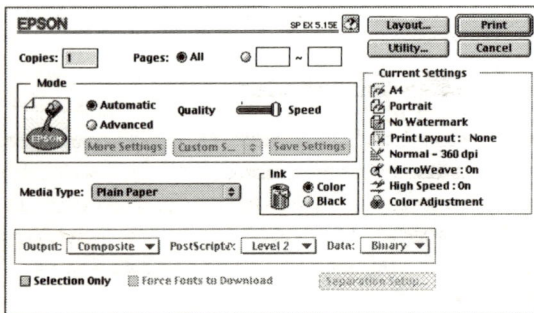

Figure 13.5 Typical set of print controls (Epson Stylus Photo EX)

Printing gradients

Gradients and blends have a tendency to band when printing. This is because they often comprise subtle tonal transitions which are difficult to reproduce in halftone.

A number of factors affect tonal transitions:

- The levels of grey in a halftone
- The amount of tonal difference in a gradient/blend
- The length of a gradient/blend
- The use of dark colours.

The levels of grey in a halftone

The levels of grey in a halftone are determined by the relationship between halftone screen ruling and outputting resolution. To ensure the maximum levels of grey (256 for each process or spot colour), the halftone screen ruling (measured in lpi) should be no more than a $^1/_{16}$ th of the imagesetter or printer resolution (measured in dpi).

For instance, if you output at 1270 dpi, the halftone screen ruling can be no higher than 79 lpi. This is too coarse for most work. By this I mean that the halftone screen dots are apparent to the naked eye. Increasing the output resolution to 2000 dpi allows you to use a halftone screen ruling of 125 lpi. This may be fine enough. But further increasing the output resolution to 2540 dpi allows you to use a halftone screen ruling of 159 lpi.

▲ Check or tick Use Printer's Default Screen in the Document Setup dialog box if you are outputting at 600 dpi or less and using a stochastic screen or other screenless system.

The amount of steps and length of a blend

When Smooth Colour spacing is specified for a blend, Illustrator creates the optimum number of steps based on the percentage of change between colours in a gradient. Illustrator calculates the number of steps using the following formula: Number of steps = 256 (assumed number of greys) × percentage change in colour.

The percentage change in colour is taken from the greatest tonal change in a colour, e.g. if Cyan changes from 90% to 20% across a blend – a change of 70% – and this change is greater than in any of the other process colours, the percentage change in colour is 0.7.

Multiplying 0.7 by 256 gives us 179.2 steps.

The number of steps determines the maximum length of a blend before banding occurs. For every 100 steps, a blend must be no greater than 76.2 mm, 216 pt or 3 inches length.

Multiplying 179.2 by 76.2 gives us a maximum length of 136.55 mm.

The use of dark colours

Whilst subtle shifts of colour spanning long distances are more likely to band than dramatic shifts across short distances, when you bring dark colours into the equation further difficulties can arise. Dark colours tend to band more than light colours and they reproduce particularly badly when blended with white. For this reason it's best to avoid their use unless blend distances are very short.

Summary

Linked images Ensure all picture links are in force on completion of artwork.

Fonts Check font usage in the Find Fonts dialog box.

Crop marks Crop marks or trim marks should be added to artworks destined for press output.

Gradients To avoid banding steer away from dark colours and long gradients combined with subtle colour shifts.

Appendix I
TYPE MEASUREMENTS

Font sizes

Fonts are sized in points (a unit measuring close to $1/72$ inch and very roughly one-third of a millimetre). A font size refers to the height of the body of a font and not the printed height (the body height can be seen when text is selected). Thus a 10 pt font has a body height of 10 pt and an overall printed height, from ascender to descender, of fractionally less.

Leading

Leading is also measured in points. Leading refers to the distance from the baseline of one line of type to the next within a paragraph (the baseline is the imaginary line running along the bottom of those letters without descenders, such as an x).

Leading is usually expressed as the sum of the font size and leading thickness. When the leading size is the same as the font size, the font is said to be unleaded. When the leading size is smaller, negative leading takes place (this would have been impossible with metal type).

Auto leading is pre-set at 120% of the font size and should be used only when initially sizing fonts or for single lines in text boxes.

Horizontal and vertical measures

Margin and gutter measures are normally specified in millimetres and paragraph indents in points. Paragraph indents are usually based on multiples or divisions of the font size, such as an em.

Spaces before paragraphs are normally measured in millimetres or points. Spaces are usually based on multiples or divisions of the leading.

Appendix II
SPECIAL CHARACTERS

Included in this appendix are the most common special characters. There are many more. If there's a character you wish to use and it's not listed, refer to Key Caps in the Apple menu on the Macintosh or to the Character Map in the Accessories folder in Windows. The Accessories folder is accessed via Windows' Start menu.

If this does not help you, you might need to buy a special font.

Most of the characters are achieved by using the modifier keys together with other keys. These keys – [⌘], [Control], [Alt] and [Shift] – should be held down separately or in various combinations whilst another key is pressed.

On the Macintosh

Quotation marks

"   [Alt]+[{ [ ]   opening double quotes

"   [Alt] [Shift]+[{ [ ]   closing double quotes

'   [Alt]+[}]]   opening single quote

'   [Alt] [Shift]+[}]]   closing single quote

Selected punctuation, characters and symbols

…   [Alt]+[: ;]   ellipsis

•   [Alt]+[* 8]   small bullet point

■   [N] (Zapf Dingbats font)   solid box

□   [N] (Zapf Dingbats, outlined)   outlined box

●	[L] (Zapf Dingbats font)	solid bullet point
○	[L] (Zapf Dingbats, outlined)	outlined bullet point
×	[Alt]+[Y] (Symbol font)	multiplication sign
fi	[Alt][Shift]+[%5]	ligature of f and i
fl	[Alt][Shift]+[^6]	ligature of f and l
©	[Alt]+[G]	copyright mark
TM	[Alt]+[@2]	trade mark
®	[Alt]+[R]	registered mark
°	[Alt][Shift]+[*8]	degree symbol
†	[Alt]+[T]	dagger
□	[Alt][Shift]+[@2]	euro
¢	[Alt]+[$4]	cent
¥	[Alt]+[Y]	yen
¿	[Alt][Shift]+[?/]	opening question mark
¡	[Alt]+[!1]	opening exclamation mark
/	[Alt][Shift]+[!1]	shallow slash for fractions

✚ The set of commands for the Euro character gives the system font. Only available from System 8.5 onwards.

Text commands

[Return]	paragraph return
[Shift]+[Return]	new line return

Hyphens and dashes

-	[-]	hyphen
–	[Alt]+[-]	en dash
—	[Alt][Shift]+[-]	em dash

Accented letters

ç   [Alt]+[C]   cedilla

é   [Alt]+[E], then [E] or other   acute

è   [Alt]+[~#], then [E] or other   grave

ü   [Alt]+[U], then [U] or other   umlaut

ñ   [Alt]+[N], then [N] or other   tilde

î   [Alt]+[I], then [I] or other   circumflex

> ❗ For all the above six commands, press the Alt key with the letter and then press the appropriate character.

In Windows

Quotation marks

"   [Alt][Shift]+[{[ ]   opening double quotes

"   [Alt][Shift]+[}]]   closing double quotes

'   [Alt]+[{[ ]   opening single quote

'   [Alt]+[}]]   closing single quote

Selected punctuation, characters and symbols

…   [Alt]+0133   ellipsis

•   [Alt][Shift]+[*8]   small bullet point

■   [N] (Wingdings font)   solid box

□   [N] (Wingdings, outlined)   outlined box

●   [L] (Wingdings font)   solid bullet point

○   [L] (Wingdings, outlined)   outlined bullet point

×   [Alt]+[Y] (Symbol font)   multiplication sign

©   [Alt][Shift]+[C]   copyright mark

TM   [Alt][Shift]+[@2]   trade mark

®	[Alt] [Shift] + [R]	registered mark
°	[Alt] +0176	degree symbol
†	[Alt] [Shift] + [T]	dagger
□	[Control] [Alt] + [$4]	euro
¢	[Alt] +0162	cent
¥	[Alt] +0165	yen
¿	[Alt] +0191	opening question mark
¡	[Alt] +0161	opening exclamation mark

✚ The set of commands for the Euro character gives the system font. This currently can be downloaded from Microsoft's web site.

Text commands

| [Return] | paragraph return |
| [Shift] + [Return] | new line return |

Hyphens and dashes

-	[- -]	hyphen
–	[Alt] + [+ =]	en dash
—	[Control] [Alt] [Shift] + [+ =]	em dash

Appendix III
GLOSSARY

Adobe Type 1 fonts PostScript technology used by font manufacturers

alert box dialog box on a screen alerting you to the consequences of a decision you are about to make

anchor point the location on a path which determines the shape and direction of the path segments extending from that location

artwork view In Illustrator, a view that displays your artwork as paths only

baseline imaginary horizontal line on which upper and lower case letters sit; descenders extend below this line

Bézier curve method of creating shapes based on mathematical methods pioneered by Pierre Bézier

bit smallest possible unit of information; short for binary digit

bitmap image image made up of pixels (or dots)

bleed defines how much of an object extending off the document page will print

body non-printing height of a font; runs from slightly above ascenders to slightly below descenders

bounding box rectangular border that appears on screen around a selected object or objects

bromide photographic paper used by imagesetters for artwork quality prints

calligraphy style of handwriting using a flat-tipped pen resulting in a stroke weight or width that varies with the direction of the line

cap the end of a stroke

character generic name for a letter, number, symbol or 'invisible'

check box small box that works as a toggle for selecting an option. (When you click on an empty box, an X or tick appears, turning it on; when you click again, the X or tick disappears and the option is turned off.)

Chooser desk accessory used to log into devices, such as printers and other computers linked to a network; also used to enable and disable AppleTalk, Apple's native networking protocol

Clipboard area of a Macintosh's memory that holds what you last cut or copied; paste inserts a copy of the current contents of the clipboard

clipping path a closed path used to partially mask objects it contains

closed path a path consisting of two or more points whose first and last points are the same

CMYK stands for cyan, magenta, yellow and key (black), the colour model used in the graphic and printing fields

column lines of type constrained within a set measure or width: in Illustrator, the content of type containers

compound path path consisting of two or more discontinuous closed paths that are treated as as single path; overlapping areas appear as a hole

crop marks lines which indicate the trimmed edge of pages

cursor Pointer or other icon indicating the screen position of the mouse

dialog box box on a screen requesting information, or a decision, from you

direction line Bézier handle controlling the shape of curves

drive floppy, removable or hard disk

drop cap large capital letter integrated within the first few lines of a paragraph

DTP short for Desktop Publishing

em measure equal to the width of the square of a font size e.g. a 15 pt em is 15 pt; corresponds roughly to the width of a capital M; used as a horizontal unit of measure – *see* en

en measure equal to half the width of the square of a font size e.g. a 15 pt en is 7.5 pt; corresponds roughly to the width of a lower-case n; used as a horizontal unit of measure – *see* em

even/odd method of filling a compound object where paths of alternating direction or winding overlap one another

field area in a dialog box or palette in which you enter values

fill colour, tint or pattern applied to the area of a path

film photographic film used by imagesetters for colour separations

fixed space word space which doesn't vary in justified alignments

flatness number of line segments PostScript uses to print a curve. High flatness values result in visibly flattened curves depending on the output device resolution

folder sub-division (sub-directory) of a disk

font single character – letter, number, punctuation mark or symbol – within a type family. Often used interchangeably with the word 'typeface'

foundry company which commissions, designs, makes and markets fonts

global colours swatches that create links with objects to which they are assigned

grabber hand tool which allows you to move around a document without using the scroll bars

grayscale depiction of grey tones between black and white; usually composed of 256 greys

greek depiction of pictures and text as blocks of grey to speed screen redraw

gutter vertical space between columns within artwork

half-tone pattern (or screen) of dots of different sizes used to simulate a continuous tone photograph, either in colour or monochrome; measured in lines per inch

hyphenation breaking of words into two parts to improve word spacing

I-beam pointer's shape when dealing with text

image graphic, photograph or illustration

imagemap bitmap image, with associated map file and program, containing multiple URL links

imagesetter digital phototypesetting machine capable of producing graphic images as well as type on bromide or film (most imagesetters are PostScript-compatible)

indent set back of lines of text in a paragraph, measured in Illustrator from the edge of the type container

insertion point blinking vertical line indicating where the next keystroke will add or delete text

join shape of a point where two segments meet at a corner

justification alignment of text at both sides of a paragraph through the adjustment of word spacing

kerning in Illustrator, inter-character spacing adjusted locally; used for styling, and optical reasons

keypad numeric keys on the right of the keyboard

keystrokes use of modifier keys with other keys to execute a command

knockout (noun) knock out (verb) option for printing where background colours do not print in areas where foreground colour overlaps; a condition where no trapping takes place

layer transparent plane that helps organize objects and controls how they stack upon each other in an artwork

leading distance between lines of text, usually measured between baselines; measured in points

line printed rule; images which contain black and white areas without intervening greys

lpi short for lines per inch; the measurement of a half-tone screen

margin outer area of the page surrounding the principal text and image areas

menu list of commands

mitre limit ratio between the length of a mitre join and the stroke width; sets the maximum length of a mitre join before it automatically converts to a bevelled join

modifier keys keys which modify the effect of a character key: standard modifier keys are [⌘], [Control], [Alt], [Shift] and [Caps Lock].

object artwork element in illustrator

open path path consisting of two or more line segments with end points which do not connect to each other

OPI short for Open Press Interface

orphan short line of text at end of paragraph positioned at the top of a column

orthogonal line line which is either horizontal or vertical

overprint option for printing where background colours print in their entirety and are not knocked out by foreground colours which overlap them

page one side of a leaf in a document

palette small movable box containing commands; range of colours

Pantone Matching System PMS for short; proprietary colour matching system used in the graphics and printing industries

paragraph any text separated by ¶

pasteboard temporary storage and work area outside the page, the contents of which don't print out

path line element comprising one or more segments

path direction direction of a closed path is defined as either clockwise or anti-clockwise; path direction is determined by where the second point is placed

photo litho short for photo lithography; the primary printing technology used in the printing industry

PICT Apple's native file format

point (of path) *see* anchor point

point unit of measure; measuring close to $^1/_{72}$ inch and very roughly one-third of a millimetre

point of origin the location used as a reference for transforming an object

PostScript device-independent page description language developed by Adobe and used by Illustrator and DTP programs

Preview in Illustrator, a view that displays your artwork as it will look when printed

process colours CMYK colours used to reproduce colour photographs and illustrations; in Illustrator, also RGB, HSB and Grayscale

profile description of the imaging performance of a computer device; used for colour management purposes

program group of instructions that tells a computer what to do; also called software

printer digital desktop or commercial device for printing or proofing documents primarily using laser, ink jet, die sublimation and thermal wax technologies

QuickDraw programming routines that enable the Macintosh to display graphic elements on screen; also used to output text and images to certain non-PostScript printers – *see* PostScript

radio buttons group of small buttons for selecting an option, only one of which can be on at any one time

raster image bitmap image

rasterize to convert vector graphics into bitmap images

registration marks marks included on film separations for purposes of accurate colour alignment

remapping rearranging the dots within a bitmap image

resolution in this book, the amount of data in a scanned image, measured in pixels (or dots) per linear inch

RGB stands for red, green, blue; the colour model used by monitors and within multimedia documents

rivers unsightly gaps running vertically between words within text

scan bitmap image created by scanner

scroll bars bars equipped with a scroll box and scroll arrows which enable you to scroll vertically or horizontally within windows

special colour *see* spot colour

spine binding edge of a document; part of a document's cover which is visible when placed on a shelf

spot colour colours other than the process colours printed as a separate colour within a photo litho printed document; sometimes called special colour

stacking order the order in which objects stack on top of one another in the same layer

stroke colour, tine or pattern applied to the outline of a path

TIFF short for Tagged Image File Format, the *de facto* file format for saving scanned images

tiling printing artwork in sections

tint lighter shade of a spot or process colour

tracking word and letter spacing adjusted locally; used for copyfitting, styling and to improve readability

transform to move, rotate, scale, shear or reflect an object

trapping technique use to minimize the effects of print misregistration

trim marks lines printed outside the edge of a document page to indicate the trimmed page size

Truetype fonts Font technology used for system fonts on both the Macintosh and PCs

typeface collection of letters, numbers, punctuation marks and symbols with an identifiable and consistent appearance. Often used interchangeably with the word 'font'

typography craft of designing with type

widow very short line of text at the end of a paragraph

width the thickness of a stroke

window enclosed area on the screen in which a document appears

wrap in Illustrator, the feature which controls the way text is displaced by objects and images

WP short for word processing

vector the numerical location of a point in terms of x and y coordinates

vector graphic drawing or object defined mathematically; sometimes called object orientated

keys

`Alt` Alt key – a modifier key used in conjunction with other keys, often providing an alternative function

`Delete` Back space/Delete key – used to delete text to the left of the insertion point, selected text and items

`⌘` Command key (with an Apple on it) – a modifier key used with other keys to issue commands; by itself on the Macintosh it activates the current selection tool when another tool is active

`Control` Control key – a modifier key used in conjunction with other keys. By itself it activates the Zoom tool; by itself in Windows it activates the current selection tool when another tool is active

`Delete` Delete key – used to delete text to the right of the insertion point

`Enter ↵` Enter key – used to close dialog boxes and implement field values, amongst other things

`Return` Return key – used to separate paragraphs, close dialog boxes and implement field values amongst other things

`Shift` Shift key – a modifier key used to capitalize letters and constrain cursor movement, amongst other things

`Tab` Tab key – keystroke which moves the insertion point to the next tab position, by default 0.5 inches apart.

INDEX